Patañjali's Yoga Sūtras

Translation - Orit Sen-Gupta

Vijnana Books
www.vijnanayoga.org

Vijnana Books
www.vijnanayoga.org

TABLE OF CONTENTS

5 Acknowledgments

7 Preface

9 Introduction to Patañjali's Yoga Sūtras

11 Note on the Translation

13 Philosophical Background to the Yoga Sūtra

19 The Translation of Basic Terms

23 The Yoga Sūtras

23 Chapter I - Samādhi Pādaḥ

45 Chapter II - Sādhana Pāda

68 Chapter III - Vibhūti Pādaḥ

93 Chapter IV - Kaivalya Pāda

109 Continuous Text: Sanskrit Transliteration and Translation

137 Continuous Text: in Devanagri script

153 Bibliography

Acknowledgements

It gives me great pleasure to thank my teachers, students and friends who helped me render this translation.

The late Father Bede Griffith of Shanti Vanam in South India, a Benedictine priest who labored tirelessly to promote understanding and tolerance between different religions, allowed me to stay in his ashram for months, provided me with a room and a typewriter, and even read my first attempts at understanding Patañjali.

The late Professor Subramacharya, Dean of Mysore University, first read the Sanskrit text with me, and encouraged me to translate it into Hebrew.

Swami Krishnananda of the Shivananda Ashram at Rishikesh, a brilliant teacher of Indian Philosophy, strengthened my resolve to study the text more profoundly. Insisting on depth of understanding and on quality, he saved me the embarrassment of publishing an unripe rendition.

Dr. Pratap taught me the Yoga-sūtra at the Kaivalyadhama Institute at Lonavla. With wonderful patience, he took the time to teach me the oral tradition, both by explanations and by setting a personal example.

Professor David Schulman, Head of the Department of Indian Studies at the Hebrew University in Jerusalem, was my Sanskrit teacher. He read the Hebrew translation, corrected a number of errors, and offered suggestions for the format of the book.

A special thanks to my daughters Dori and Mira who inspire our family with their energy and optimism.

Jerusalem, 1994

Originally I translated the Yoga Sūtras into Hebrew as there was no translation of it available to the Israeli public. Since there were so many translations into English, it seemed to me unnecesary to attempt an English version. Finally, in 1997, for the sake of the international teachers' training that was held in Berkeley, California with Dona Holleman, I translated this brief work into English and composed a short introduction. I never published it, but rather used it informally for studying Patañjali in the teacher trainings. It is only now, many years later, with publishing made simple, that I am printing this work, in the hope that it will be useful for yoga practitioners.

I want to thank Aaron Chankin for learning the Sanskrit font, integrating it into the manuscript, and then working with me to better the understanding of this wonderful, ancient text.

Orit Sen-gupta, October 2013, Jerusalem

Preface

One night in 1981, in Benares, India, I was inspired to make a decision that resulted in the translation before you. The decision was to change the direction of my studies and learn Sanskrit in order to read the ancient yoga texts in the original. I was filled with excitement, even though I had no idea what was in store for me. The language of Sanskrit, I must admit, was more difficult for me that the language of Yoga. Nonetheless, when I started to read the beloved texts in the original, I was thrilled. Through the structure and usage of the language I had the feeling I was coming closer to understanding the amazing phenomena that had attracted me in years past to the wonderful world of Yoga.

Yoga is an ancient culture that comprises many layers and embraces many approaches. Despite its rich past, however, its history has not been documented consistently.

The assumption at the root of the yogic outlook is that the source of suffering is not-knowing, or *avidyā*. The root of the Sanskrit word *avidyā* is "*vid*" to know, and its parrarel in Latin is "*videre*" is to see. *Avidyā* implies the inability to see reality as it is. Translated usually as 'ignorance', yoga's response to this inability to percieve or know reality is to give individuals the means by which they can see reality clearly. Like Plato, the old Yogis thought that when a person grasps reality as it is, he will always choose to do the right thing at the right time.

The question then arises: how does one reach this pure and precise seeing? The Yogis believed that in order to percieve well, one must first aquire an intimate knowledge of the 'seeing apparatus' and its ways of functioning. Then it is to be cleaned as one would wipe away dirt from eyeglasses and polish the lenses. When the mind through this process becomes luminous and transparent, it will reflect reality precisely as it is. Unlike other philosophical systems where the intellect is of primary importance, in yoga the practices are directed to the whole person, body, mind and heart.

The yogic way, which combined the search for true seeing with a search for ethical and personal excellence, lent yoga its intensity and uniqueness. Gradually, its practice spread throughout the Indian subcontinent. Later, via Buddhism, it was transported to the Far East and flourished there, having a considerable influence within the various cultures. In the 19th century, yoga arrived in Europe and North America as well.

Yoga was usually known by its main technique of meditation, or *dhyāna* in Sanskrit. In China it was called Chan and in Japan, Zen. Meditation is a technique that empowers the physical and mental aspects of an individual and allows for unmediated experiences of high states of consciousness that usually occur only during moments of grace. Because of these, yoga attracted the elite of Hindu culture and afterwards the intellectual elites in other countries as well.

But yoga survived also due to its universalism; yoga is not a religion, but a technique for rekindling and intensifying spiritual potential. In addition, yoga is not based on blind faith, but on experience. For these reasons, it can easily be integrated into many social systems and resonate with manifold cultures and beliefs, without posing a threat.

Introduction to Patañjali's Yoga-Sūtra

Who was Patañjali? Actually, not much is known about him. Ancient Indian tradition maintains he is the same Patañjali who lived around 200 BCE, and wrote a commentary to the renowned grammar book by Pāṇini. Other researchers, because of the nature of the content and because of some of the terminology in the text, believe that Patañjali was a different person who lived in the first or second century CE.

According to Hindu mythology, the thousand-headed serpent, wishing to teach yoga on earth, fell (*pat*) out of heaven into the hands (*añjali*) of a virtuous woman who had prayed to have a son, and thus received his name: *Patañjali.*

All we know about Patañjali is based on his writings alone. He cannot really be called the father of yoga, since, as we already made clear, the sources of yoga are very ancient. He was, however, a gifted editor who was able to combine the philosophy of yoga with its wide array of techniques, formulating both into a unified and terse text. Perhaps because of its quality and comprehensive nature, the text was of immense influence. In fact, the Patañjali Sūtras became one of the six *darśanas* (schools of thought) of Indian philosophy, quoted in many places, and on which many commentaries have been written.

Each of the six *darśanas* is written in *sūtra* form. The sentences in the Yoga Sūtras are brief, and the meaning often obscure. They were meant to be recited from memory, and their meaning was probably passed on orally from teacher to disciple. Due to the brevity of the writing and its cryptic nature, the Yoga Sūtras were studied with the aid of commentaries. These commentaries cannot with certainty be regarded as elucidating Patañjali, since even the first and most famous of them, that of Vyāsa, was written only in the 4th or 5th century CE. Most commentators did not belong to Patañjali's school, and were scholars and not yogis. Nonetheless, students of Patañjali's sūtras should eventually read Vyāsa, since all subsequent commentaries refer to his comments, accept him as an authority, and see him as a disciple of Patañjali's school of thought. He is in his own right a brilliant student and teacher of yoga.

Through his writing, Patañjali is revealed not only as a gifted editor, but also as a Yogi. The sūtras are filled with knowledge, wisdom, and modesty. For example, after Patañjali presents us with various techniques for cultivating *samādhi*, a high state of consciousness, he ends with a simple sūtra that says: "*Or by meditation, as desired.*"

Although his writings depict a chart in which paths to certain areas of consciousness are delineated, an opening is always left for additional and unknown side trails.

Note on the Translation

I would like to clarify a number of facts about Sanskrit before we approach the translated text of the Yoga Sūtra.

Sanskrit is a very rich and colorful language, both in vocabulary and in the grammatical structures it permits. In Sanskrit, as in some European languages, the word endings imply their syntax.

At the time in which the text was written, Sanskrit was not a spoken language. It was kept alive and taught as a literary language studied by *paṇḍits* (scholars). The writing was well thought out and very accurate, especially in view of the fact that it was intended for study and oral recitation.

The tendency in Sanskrit to use verbs in their passive form gives a sense of another kind of reality where time is slower and the individual instead of feeling a creator of his reality, feels shaped by it. Every language is structured uniquely, in a manner that stems from the perception of reality in the culture in which the language was formed. Parallel terms do not always exist between languages. This is especially evident when reading Patañjali's sūtras. For many years Indian culture was introspective, turned towards understanding the structure of human consciousness. A detailed terminology was developed for different states of consciousness, and these terms were used to explain how one perceives reality and responds to it.

The difficulty in translation is in maintaining something of the original structure and rhythm of the language, and establishing a terminology for the states of consciousness. To this is added the fact that the text is difficult to understand in the first place, even in its original language, and was therefore studied with the aid of commentaries in India itself. In this manner perhaps some clarity was achieved, but I suspect that at times Patañjali's intention was lost in the verbosity and viewpoints of his commentators. For this reason, I felt the need to refocus on the text itself, and it is presented here with no commentary other than the necessary introduction. In translating, I have tried to adhere to the original as much as possible, in syntax and in the grammatical roots. This does not make the reading easier, but it gives the reader access to the source and a view of the world of yoga through the eyes of Patañjali, who is considered the father of classical yoga.

Philosophical Background to the Yoga Sūtra

In the yoga texts which preceded the *Yoga Sūtras*, such as the *Upaniṣads*, the *Bhagavad-Gītā* and so forth, the concept that goes hand-in-hand with the Yoga techniques is *vedānta. Vedānta* is a philosophy that believes in a single reality that is essentially spiritual. This reality is multifaceted or dual only in the consciousness of one who is blind to its oneness. In the yogic traditions that arose after Patañjali's sūtras, there is a resurgence of the non-dualistic concept of *vedānta*.

Positioned between these two periods, Patañjali offers a **dualistic** concept of reality. Leaning on the ancient dualistic philosophy of Sāṃkhya, the Yoga Sūtras do not accept the idea that nature or phenomena called in Sanskrit *prakṛti*, the Seen, is only an aspect of the Self, the *puruṣa*, the Seer. From the point of view of Patañjali's yoga philosophy, *puruṣa* (the Seer) and *prakṛti* (the Seen) are two entirely separate entities that exist independently of one another.

A third concept, without which we cannot understand the connection between the Seer and the Seen is *citta*, consciousness. It is defined as the subtle aspect of *prakriti*, the Seen, and it is also the function within us onto which the sights and sounds of the world are projected, so it sees too.

In order to assist the reader, I would like to present the the sūtras that discuss each of these terms, *puruṣa, prakṛti* and *citta*, and explain a bit more about them.

Puruṣa - the Seer, the Self

During the period in which the Yoga Sūtras were written, the term *puruṣa* - the Seer or the "Self," was known. Perhaps this is the reason Patañjali explains the term only partially. Another reason may be that by its very nature, *puruṣa* is always the Seer or knower, and so, by its very nature, it cannot be seen. Not being an object, it is forever elusive. In Sāṃkhya it is described by inductive reasoning: "Because the world exists, a world which we can see and discuss, we must assume a Seer." Nonetheless, one can understand the principal meaning of *puruṣa* from the sūtras. *Puruṣa* is primarly the Seer, without change, and utterly undiluted. Although pure, it can perceive notions. It is just seeing.

It is important to note that this definition is no abstract spiritual ideal, but a term that reflects a yogic experience. We must therefore not hold on to the term itself, but rather aspire to understand the experience that brought about the establishment of the term. According to the Yogis, *abiding in the Seer* is the ultimate goal.

The following verses, though cryptic both in the original Sanskrit and in translation, introduce the reader to the way the term *puruṣa* is slowly revealed in the text, and assist in the development of a broad notion of its difficult-to-grasp essence.

I.3 Then the dwelling of the Seer in his own form.

I.16 The superior one (detachment) is by perceiving the Self, *puruṣa*; then there is no thirst for the *guṇa* (nature's inherent qualities).

II.20 The Seer who is (but) seeing, although pure, perceives notions.

III.35 Pleasure, *(bhoga)* is a notion that does not distinguish between *puruṣa* and harmonious mind, *sattva*. By *saṃyama* (intense meditation) on its own form, and the purpose of another, knowledge of *puruṣa*.

III.49 By merely knowing to distinguish between harmonious mind, *sattva*, and *puruṣa*, supremacy over all states of existence and all knowledge.

III.55 When the harmonious mind, *sattva* and the *puruṣa* are of the same purity *kaivalya* (aloneness).

IV.18 The fluctuations (*vṛttis)* of the consciousness are always known to their master, the *puruṣa*, which is unchanging.

Prakṛti, the Seen - Phenomena, Nature,

Puruṣa is the Seer, and *prakṛti*, all of phenomena or nature, is what is seen. All that is Seen is continually changing and oscillating through three main qualities or *guṇas*: harmony *(sattva)*, movement *(rajas)* and heaviness *(tamas)*. These three states, elaborated below, exist mostly in combination; rarely do they appear in pure form.

Prakṛti (nature) has a hierarchical structure:

1. At the basis is *aliṅga* - "without sign" - the hidden potential of existence (for example, a man and woman who have not yet met).
2. Second is *liṅga* - "with sign" - the realization of potential (in this example, the man and woman meet and have sexual intercourse).
3. Next is *aviśṣa* - "non-distinct" - the creation of the possibility for uniqueness and the creation of conditions for the action of the senses (the sperm fertilizes the ovum and, yet unseen, fetus is formed).
4. Finally, *viśṣa* - "distinct" - this stage can already be seen (here mind is formed, then the senses and five elements: the baby).

The first three conditions are hidden; and only in the fourth, that of *viśṣa* - that of uniqueness - is the universe formed in actuality.
The purpose of the world is *bhoga (*pleasure) and liberation.
Prakṛti, nature, is not only a mechanical being, but encompasses within it consciousness - *citta* - the sixth sense, and perhaps it is here that a meeting ensues between the two poles of *puruṣa* and *prakṛti*.
A selection of sūtras pertaining to *prakṛti* is provided to introduce the reader to its presentation in the Yoga Sūtras:

II.18. The Seen has the characteristics of brightness, action, and stability - it has the nature of the elements and the senses and its purpose is, *bhoga* (pleasure) and liberation.

II.19 The divisions of the qualities, *guṇas* are distinct, not distinct, with sign and without sign.

II.21 The soul of the Seen is for that purpose only.

II.22 Although for him whose purpose is fulfilled it disappears, it still hasn't disappeared for others since it is (the) common-experience.

IV.2 The transformation into another type of existence [is possible] because of Nature's abundance.

IV.3 The instrumental cause does not impel Nature's [evolving]; it only removes obstacles as the farmer [irrigates his field].

Citta - Consciousness

Citta, consciousness, is a function within us that registars all the intake of the senses and then integrates it with what we already know, to give us a picture of what is happening. In this sense, consciousness, while not the Seer, clearly functions as a seeing apperatus. Since consciousness and its contents can be seen and reflected upon, it is understood in yoga philosophy as part of *prakṛti*, the Seen.

Citta is one of the key terms of the Yoga Sūtras and appears in the text 22 times, more than any other term.

The uniqueness of consciousness is that through it we perceive both *prakṛti* - Nature, the world; and, as the text will hint, through it, we can come closer to *puruṣa* - the Seer.

Patañjali says (VI.17): "Depending on consciousness's hope of being colored by it, a thing is known or not known," explaining that we actually never meet an objective reality but only a subjective one that is constructed along the lines of our wishes.

When consciousness becomes refined, and turns to the Highest, its *puruṣa*, it reflects *puruṣa* and undergoes a transformation.

This then is the drama: The *citta* discovers nature - the world, and then slowly discovers not only the pleasures, but the pain and suffering as well - the continual change. When it becomes sated with the world, it seeks out another way of being, finally returning to the Seer, the source of its seeing.

The *Yoga Sūtras* form a map drawn for the sake of a consciousness that yearns to meet its deepest self. Thus it guides us to hidden paths that lead to *puruṣa*.

1. In our ordinary states of mind, the eyes of the consciousness are turned towards the phenomena of the world

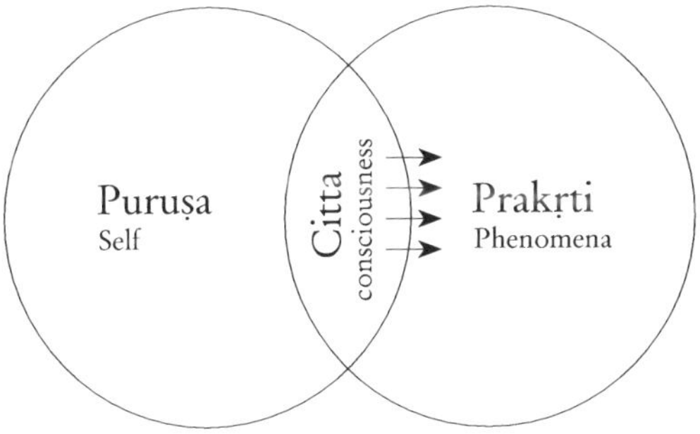

2. The practice of yoga trains the consciousness to turn inwardly towards its true Self, the Puruṣa

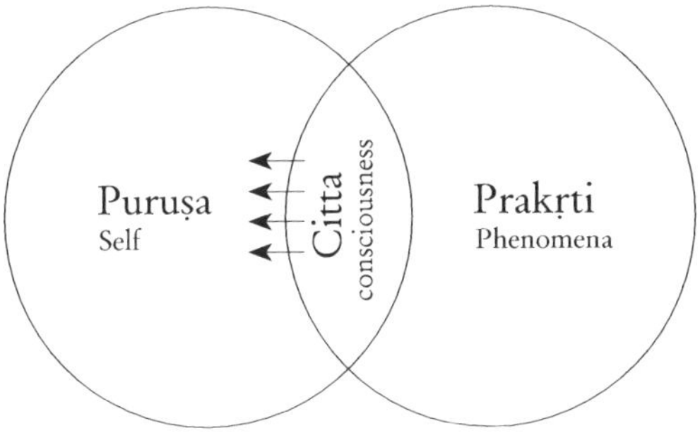

A selection of sūtras pertaining to *citta* is provided to introduce the reader to the context in which it appears in Patañjali's yoga.

I.2 Yoga is restraining the activities of the consciousness.

I.30 Disease, apathy, doubt, carelessness, laziness, dissipation, erring vision, not reaching the stages [of *samādhi*], and instability [in them]: these are the distractions of consciousness, these are the obstacles.

I.33 Cultivating friendliness, kindness, gladness, and equanimity towards objects of joy, suffering, merit, or demerit [brings about] calmness of the consciousness.

I.37 Or consciousness has objects free of attachment.

II.54 *Pratyāhāra* [sense withdrawal] is as if the senses are imitating the true form of consciousness, by disuniting from their objects.

III.1 Binding the consciousness to a place is Concentration.

III.9 The imprints, *saṃskāras* of emergence disappear and the *saṃskāras* of restraint come outdoors. Then a moment of restraint of the consciousness.

III.11 When all objectives diminish and one-pointedness rises up in the consciousness, then the *samādhi* of Transformation.

III.19 By [direct perception] of [another's] notion - the knowledge of his consciousness.

III.34 [By *saṃyama*] on the heart - the understanding of consciousness.

III.38 By relaxing the causes of bondage, and a feeling of passing through, consciousness can enter another's body.

IV.4 Created consciousness results from 'I am'ness only.

IV.5 There are distinct activities, yet it is one consciousness that impels the many.

IV.15 While the thing [remains] the same, consciousness(es) are different; therefore the paths of these are different.

IV.17 Depending on consciousness's expectation of being colored by it, a thing is known or not known.

IV.18 The activities of the consciousness are always known to its master, the *puruṣa*, that is unchanging.

IV.23 When the consciousness is colored by the Seer and the Seen [it perceives] all objectives.

IV.26 Then consciousness is pulled towards *viveka* (discernment) and leans towards Aloneness.

The Translation of Basic Terms

Some Sanskrit terms are particularly difficult to translate. Below, further explanations are offered to clarify the choices made in the translation.

Terms Describing Reality

Puruṣa - is translated into English as "*person*" or "*Self*". Puruṣa signifies the individual self but also the transcendental primary Self.
Prakṛti - this term is usually understood as signifying nature, the material and intellectual cosmic phenomena. It is translated as "*Nature*" or "*the world.*"

Terms of Consciousness

There are many terms describing states of consciousness in Sanskrit; three are mentioned in the Yoga Sūtra: *citta*, *manas* and *buddhi*.
Citta - originates from the root *cit*, to be aware. I chose to translate this term as "*consciousness.*" In some texts it appears as "*mind.*"
Manas - originates from the root *man* - to think. According to the ancient texts, it is this part of the consciousness that is responsible for thought and feelings. I translate this term as "*mind.*"
Buddhi - originates from the root *budh* - to be awake and aware. It is from this same root that the name of the great religion *Buddhism* comes. According to the classic Hindi commentaries, *buddhi* is the highest and clearest intelligence in the consciousness. I used the term "*awareness*" in this translation.

Terms of Knowledge

Avidyā - from the root *vid* - to know; *a*-non; therefore meaning *not-knowing*. This term, one of the basic concepts of yogic philosophy, is usually translated as *ignorance*. Although *vidyā* refers to worldly knowledge, the term *avidyā* gained a more spiritual meaning, and must be understood as a state of ignorance regarding the spiritual perception of reality. It is translated here as "*not-knowing.*"
Jñana - originating from the root *jña* - to know. This term is

different from the term *vidyā*, and I used either "*knowledge*" or "*wisdom,*" according to the context.
Prajña - (*pra+jña*) means "*transcendental wisdom.*"

Additional terms pertaining to Consciousness

According to the yogic perception of consciousness, a number of elements are active in consciousness itself, the first of which is *saṃskāra*.

Saṃskāras - imprints, originates from the root *sams* + *kṛ* - to do. The *saṃskāras* are stored memories in our consciousness that are created at each encounter with the reality that surrounds us from the moment we are born. Each encounter with the essential reality is imprinted on our brain. When something in the surrounding reality touches us and awakens a deep memory, this imprint surfaces into our consciousness and formulates a reaction.

Vāsanās - impressions, are inherent character traits that influence our attitude towards reality. Unlike the *saṃskāras* (imprints) that are continually created and originate in the relatively recent past, the *vāsanās* are printed from the very distant past, from antiquity.

Nirodha - restraining, is a central term in the text, originating from the root *rudh* and translated "*to restrict, suppress, stop.*" *Nirodha* includes in it a whole process, beginning with restraining and constraining, all the way to stopping, as if describing the process of braking, where there can be a slowing or partial stopping up to a complete halt.

Kaivalya - aloneness is a term originating from the word *kevala* - alone. *Kaivalya* relates to an exclusive and continual vision of the Seer, the Self. At the end of a spiritual journey, from which there is no turning back, a reality of exclusive vision is formed. This is the "aloneness" of the Self.

Untranslatable Terms

I have chosen not to translate a number of terms in the text, since I could not find words to convey their meaning, and because they are basic terms in yoga philosophy.

Karma - fate, and also actions. The sum of all the actions a person performs in life in accordance with fate, and the effect it has on the way he functions and on what happens to him.

Dharma - natural law. Everything and everyone has his own *dharma*, the right way of living. According to Indian tradition, it is better to live one's own *dharma*, even if it is inferior, rather than live someone else's *dharma*.

Samādhi - the eighth term in *Aṣṭāṅga Yoga. Samādhi* is the highest state of consciousness, with varying degrees of intensity, and is a technique of unification. The source of the word is in the root *sam+a+dha* - putting together. Since it is difficult to translate, and has no parallel term in other languages, it is usually left untranslated.

Guṇa - three main qualities or building blocks that make up all phenomena.

The qualities of phenomena are termed *guṇas* in Sanskrit. The world is in a state of continual change, moving between these three *guṇas* and the shades yielded when they are combined.

- *Sattva* - purity, whiteness, lightness, cleanliness, serenity.
- *Rajas* - activity, redness, disquiet, lack of order, anger.
- *Tamas* - stability, darkness, laziness, filth, indifference.

Sattva - one of the three gunas. In this text the term sattva is used at times to designate 'buddhi', (the highest form of consciousness within us) in its most pure and lucid state.

Saṃyama - intensive focusing that is a combination of concentration, meditation and *samādhi*. It is a process of intensifying concentration and meditation, first focused on external objects, followed by introspection on *puruṣa* until achieving *the highest Samādhi*.

A Note on Pronunciation

The following is a partial guide to the pronunciation of Sanskrit transliteration.

Vowels:		example:
a	like the u in hut	jñāna, āsana
ā	like the a in father	samādhi, abhāva
e	like the e in egg	etena, upekṣa
i	like the i in sit	nirodha, ahiṃsā
ī	like the ee in sleep	īśvara, grahītṛ
u	like the u in put	buddhi, guṇa
ū	like the oo in hoot	pūrva, mūla
ṛ	like the ri in rich	vṛtti, prakṛti
ai	like the i in smile	kaivalya, vaira
au	like the ou in house	bhaumā, sthitau
o	like the o in home	bhoga, āloka

Consonants:	example:
kh like the kh in bunkhouse	duḥkha, sukha
gh like the gh in loghouse	laghu
ṅ like the ng in king	aṅga
c like the ch in chair	citta, cakra
ch like the ch-h in coach-horse	chid
th like the th in pothole	artha, kathaṃtā
dh like the dh in madhouse	dharma, dhyānā
ph like the ph in topheavy	phala
bh like the bh in Clubhouse	abhyāsa, bhoga
ś and ṣ like the sh in ship	kleśa, puruṣa

ṭ, ṭh, ḍ, ḍh and ṇ are pronounced by bringing the lower surface of the tongue against the roof of the palate. examples: draṣṭṛ, pratiṣṭhā, nāḍi, rūḍha, guṇa

In general, syllables with long vowels (ā, ī, ū, ṛ) are accented and stressed, as in bhāvana, tīvra, sva-rūpa, or vṛtti.

The Yoga Sūtras

2 MIN - LEARNING CD

समाधिपादः Chapter I - Samādhi Pādaḥ

समाधि samādhi = from sam + a + √dha, 'putting together'; 'sam' and 'a' are prefixes, √dha is the root (see page 21).
पाद pāda = chapter

• NOW - NOT SOON - NOT LATER. SRI PAT. IS CALLING ATTENTION

अथ योगानुशासनम् ॥ १ । १ ॥
I.1. atha-yoga-anuśāsanam
Now the instruction of yoga.

• HE WAS NOT CLAIMING IT WAS A NEW TEACHING • JUST A DIFFERENT WAY OF EXPLAINING

अथ atha = now
योग yoga = from √yuj, 'to yoke, to join together'
अनुशासन anuśāsana = instruction (from anu + √śās) - anu is the prefix and śās is the root; √śās - 'to teach, to instruct'

योगश्चित्तवृत्तिनिरोधः ॥ १ । २ ॥
I.2. yogaś-citta-vṛtti-nirodhaḥ
Yoga is restraining the vṛttis of consciousness.

HEART OF RAJA YOGA. THIS COULD BE PRACTICED FOR A LIFETIME.

योग yoga = (see I.1)
चित्त citta = mind, consciousness (from √cit, 'to observe, to be attentive to')
वृत्ति vṛtti = activity, movement, function, wave (from √vṛt, 'to turn, to whirl')
निरोध nirodha = restraining (from ni + √rudh, 'to restrain, to restrict, to suppress, to stop')

तदा द्रष्टुः स्वरूपेऽवस्थानम् ॥ १ । ३ ॥
I.3. tadā draṣṭuḥ sva-rūpe'vasthānam
Then the dwelling of the 'see'er in his own form.

तदा tadā = then
द्रष्टृ draṣṭṛ = Seer. The genitive of √dṛś, 'to see', literally 'see'er. This term in Patañjali is puruṣa, the eternal spirit in man/woman.
स्वरूप sva-rūpa = own form. This term will occur many times in the sūtras. In the yogic language essence and truth are expressed by the term 'form' - rūpa.
अवस्थान avasthāna = abiding, dwelling (from ava + √sthā, 'to stand')

वृत्तिसारूप्यमितरत्र ॥ १ । ४ ॥
I.4. vṛtti-sārūpyam-itaratra
Otherwise the same form as the vṛttis [is taken by the 'See'er].

वृत्ति vṛtti = activity, movement, function, wave (see I.2)
सारूप्य sārūpya = sameness or similarity of form, likeness (from sa + √rūpa, 'form')
इतरत्र itaratra = otherwise

वृत्तयः पञ्चतयः क्लिष्टाक्लिष्टाः ॥ १ । ५ ॥
I.5. vṛttayaḥ pañcatayaḥ kliṣṭa-akliṣṭāḥ
The vṛttis are fivefold distressing, [and] not distressing.

वृत्ति vṛtti = activity, movement, function, wave (see I.2)
पञ्चतय pañca-taya = fivefold (from pañca, 'five')
क्लिष्ट kliṣṭa = distressing (from √kliś, 'to torment, trouble, cause pain, suffering; afflicted, distressed')
अक्लिष्ट akliṣṭa = not distressing (from a + kliṣṭa)

प्रमाणविपर्ययविकल्पनिद्रास्मृतयः ॥ १ । ६ ॥

I.6. pramāṇa-viparyaya-vikalpa-nidrā-smṛtayaḥ

[They are] valid cognition, misconception, imagination (mental construction), sleep and memory.

प्रमाण pramāṇa = valid cognition, knowledge, right measure (from pra + √mā, 'to measure, estimate')
विपर्यय viparyaya = misconception (from vi + pari + √i, 'to go')
विकल्प vikalpa = imagination, mental construction (from vi + √kḷp)
This term literally means 'between kalpas (worlds)'; in yogic literature it means a fancy or imagination, something unreal that doesn't exist in the world.
निद्रा nidrā = sleep (from ni + √drā, 'to sleep')
स्मृति smṛti = memory (from √smṛ, 'to remember')

प्रत्यक्षानुमानागमाः प्रमाणानि ॥ १ । ७ ॥

I.7. pratyakṣa-anumāna-āgamāḥ pramāṇāni

Valid cognitions [are founded upon] perception, inference and testimony.

प्रत्यक्ष pratyakṣa = perception, direct seeing (from prati + √akṣa, 'eye')
अनुमान anumāna = inference (from anu + √mā, 'to measure')
आगम āgama = testimony (from ā + √gam, 'to go')
In the classical commentaries this is understood not as testimony in the usual sense, but as the testimony of tradition (texts and teachers).
प्रमाण pramāṇa = valid cognition, knowledge, right measure (see I.6)

विपर्ययो मिथ्याज्ञानमतद्रूपप्रतिष्ठम् ॥ १ । ८ ॥
I.8. viparyayo mithyā-jñānam-atad-rūpa-pratiṣṭham
Misconception is false knowledge not based on the real form of that [object].

विपर्यय viparyaya = misconception (see I.6)
मिथ्या mithyā = incorrect, false
ज्ञान jñāna = knowledge (from the verb √jña, 'to know', parallel to 'gnosis')
अतद् a-tad = not that, or not this
रूप rūpa = form (see I.3)
प्रतिष्ठा pratiṣṭhā = based, grounded in (from prati + √sthā, 'to stand')

शब्दज्ञानानुपाती वस्तुशून्यो विकल्पः ॥ १ । ९ ॥
I.9. śabda-jñāna-anupātī vastu-śūnyo vikalpaḥ
Mental construction or Imagination follows word knowledge and is empty of [actual] objects.

शब्द śabda = sound, word
ज्ञान jñāna = knowledge
अनुपातिन् anupātin = follows (from anu + √pat, 'to fall')
वस्तु vastu = object, thing (from √vas, 'to abide, remain')
शून्य śūnya = empty, devoid (from √śvi, 'swollen')
विकल्प vikalpa = imagination, mental construction (see I.6)

अभावप्रत्ययालम्बना वृत्तिर्निद्रा ॥ १ । १० ॥
I.10. abhāva-pratyaya-ālambanā vṛttir-nidrā
Sleep is a vṛtti supported by the notion of non-becoming.

अभाव abhāva = non-becoming (from a + √bhū, 'to be')
प्रत्यय pratyaya = notion (from prati + √i, 'to go')
आलम्बन ālambana = support (from ā + √lamb, 'to hang from, to support, to hold')
वृत्ति vṛtti = activity, movement, function, wave (see I.2)
निद्रा nidrā = sleep (see I.6)

अनुभूतविषयासंप्रमोषः स्मृतिः ॥ १ । ११ ॥

I.11. anubhūta-viṣaya-asaṃpramoṣaḥ smṛtiḥ

Memory is not letting drop the experienced object.

अनुभूत anubhūta = experienced, apprehended (from anu + √bhū, 'to be')
विषय viṣaya = object, sphere (from √viṣ, 'to be active' + aya)
असंप्रमोष asaṃpramoṣa = not letting drop (from a + sam + pra + √muṣ, 'to steal, take away from')
स्मृति smṛti = memory (see I.6)

अभ्यासवैराग्याभ्यां तन्निरोधः ॥ १ । १२ ॥

I.12. abhyāsa-vairāgyābhyāṃ tan-nirodhaḥ

Those are restrained by practice and non-attachment (detachment, dispassion).

अभ्यास abhyāsa = practice (from abhi + √ās, 'to concentrate one's attention, practice, exercise, study')
वैराग्य vairāgya = non-attachment (from vai + √raj, 'excited, attracted, passionate')
तद् tad = that; here: 'those'
निरोध nirodha = restraining (see I.2)

तत्र स्थितौ यत्नोऽभ्यासः ॥ १ । १३ ॥

I.13. tatra sthitau yatno'bhyāsaḥ

Practice is the effort of becoming stable there.

तत्र tatra = there
स्थिति sthiti = standing, remaining, steadiness, stability (from √sthā, 'to stand')
यत्न yatna = effort (from √yat, 'to exert one's self, endeavor; to strive')
अभ्यास abhyāsa = practice (see I.12)

स तु दीर्घकालनैरन्तर्यसत्कारासेवितो दृढभूमिः ॥ १ । १४ ॥

I.14. sa tu dīrgha-kāla-nairantarya-satkāra-āsevito dṛḍha-bhūmiḥ

But this [practice] becomes firmly grounded when done intensively, properly and continuously over a long period.

स sa = it; here: this (from tad)
तु tu = but (This is to emphasize that a correctly done practice that is maintained continuously for a long time is not obvious.)
दीर्घ dīrgha = long
काल kāla = time
नैरन्तर्य nairantarya = continuously
सत्कार satkāra = well-done; here: 'properly' (from sat - 'well, right' + √kṛ, 'to do')
आसेवित āsevita = performed intensively (from ā + √sev, 'to perform with zeal')
दृढ dṛḍha = firmly (from √dṛṃh, 'to fasten')
भूमि bhūmi = earth; here: 'grounded' (from √bhū, 'to be')

दृष्टानुश्रविकविषयवितृष्णस्य वशीकारसंज्ञा वैराग्यम् ॥ १ । १५ ॥

I.15. dṛṣṭa-ānuśravika-viṣaya-vitṛṣṇasya vaśīkāra-saṃjñā vairāgyam

Vairāgya (non-attachment) is the clear-knowledge of mastery of one who is not thirsty for objects seen or heard.

दृष्ट dṛṣṭa = seen (from √dṛś, 'to see')
आनुश्रविक ānuśravika = heard (from anu + √śru, 'to hear')
विषय viṣaya = object (see I.11)
वितृष्ण vitṛṣṇa = not thirsty (from vi + √tṛṣ, 'to thirst')
वशीकार vaśīkāra = mastery
संज्ञा saṃjñā = clear-knowledge (from sam + √jña, 'to know')
वैराग्य vairāgya = non-attachment (see I.12)

तत्परं पुरुषख्यातेर्गुणवैतृष्ण्यम् ॥ १ । १६ ॥

I.16. tat-paraṃ puruṣa-khyāter-guṇa-vaitṛṣṇyam

The superior of that (non-attachment) is by perceiving puruṣa; then there is no thirst for the guṇas.[1]

तद् tad = that

पर para = superior

पुरुष puruṣa = person, Self

ख्याति khyāti = to perceive, to have vision (from √khyā, 'to know')

गुण guṇa = (see footnote)

वैतृष्ण्य vaitṛṣṇya = no thirsting [after] (see vitṛṣṇa, I.15)

वितर्कविचारानन्दास्मितानुगमात्संप्रज्ञातः ॥ १ । १७ ॥

I.17. vitarka-vicāra-ānanda-asmitā-anugamāt-saṃprajñātaḥ[2]

Wisdom [Samādhi] is accompanied by thought, reflection, bliss and 'I am'ness[3].

वितर्क vitarka = thought, supposition, doubt, uncertainty (from vi + √tark, 'to think, to ponder')

विचार vicāra = reflection, deliberation, consideration (from vi + √car, 'to move')

आनन्द ānanda = bliss, ecstasy, joy, delight (from ā + √nand, 'to rejoice, delight')

अस्मिता asmitā = asmi, 'I am' + tā, 'ness': literally - 'I am'ness

---

1 ***Guṇas*** - three main building blocks that make up all matter:
- *Sattva* - purity, whiteness, lightness, cleanliness, serenity, lucidity
- *Rajas* - activity, redness, disquiet, lack of order, anger
- *Tamas* - stability, darkness, laziness, filth, indifference

The qualities of phenomena are termed *guṇas* in Sanskrit. The world is in a state of continual change, moving between the states and the shades of their combinations.

2 In some editions, this sutra is written with the addition of the word 'rūpa' (form): वितर्कविचारानन्दास्मितारूपानुगमात्संप्रज्ञातः । vitarka-vicāra-ānanda-asmitā-rūpa-anugamāt-saṃprajñātaḥ

3 Wisdom Samādhi - Saṃprajñāta in Sanskrit is a technical name for samādhi in which there are objects, outer or inner, which engross the practitioner. In asaṃprajñāta Samādhi there are no objects whatsoever. This issue will be expanded towards the end of the first chapter.

अनुगम anugama = going along with, following, accompanying (from anu + √gam, 'to go')
संप्रज्ञात saṃprajñāta = see footnote (from sam + √prajñā, 'transcendental wisdom)

विरामप्रत्ययाभ्यासपूर्वः संस्कारशेषोऽन्यः ॥ १ । १८ ॥
I.18. virāma-pratyaya-abhyāsa-pūrvaḥ saṃskāra-śeṣo'nyaḥ
The other [Samādhi][4] is preceded by practicing the notion of ceasing. It has a residue only of saṃskāras[5].

विराम virāma = cessation, termination (from vi + √ram, 'to stop')
प्रत्यय pratyaya = notion (see I.10)
अभ्यास abhyāsa = practice (see I.12)
पूर्व pūrva = former, earlier, prior, preceding; first, initial
संस्कार saṃskāra = [mental] imprint (see footnote) (from + √kṛ, 'to do')
शेष śeṣa = remainder, residue (from √śiṣ, 'to remain, to be left')
अन्य anya = other

भवप्रत्ययो विदेहप्रकृतिलयानाम् ॥ १ । १९ ॥
I.19. bhava-pratyayo videha-prakṛti-layānām
Bhava-pratyaya [Samādhi] is of the bodiless and those absorbed in Prakṛti.

भव bhava = becoming, birth, origin, being, state of being (from √bhū, 'to be')
प्रत्यय pratyaya = notion (see I.10)

4 This is Asaṃprajñāta, samādhi without object or seed. It is considered the most intense level of Samādhi. Sūtras 18-20 deal with it.

5 Saṃskāras are stored memories in our consciousness that are created at each meeting with the reality that surrounds us from the moment we are born. Each meeting with the essential reality is imprinted on our brain. When something in the surrounding reality touches us and awakens a deep memory, this imprint surfaces into our consciousness and formulates a reaction. (See also Vāsanās, footnote II.1)

विदेह videha = bodiless (from vi + √dih, 'to cover'; देह deha = body)
प्रकृति prakṛti = nature (from pra + √kṛ, 'to do')
लय laya = dissolution, absorption (from √lī - 'to melt, dissolve; to lie')

श्रद्धावीर्यस्मृतिसमाधिप्रज्ञापूर्वक इतरेषाम् ॥ १ । २० ॥
I.20. śraddhā-vīrya-smṛti-samādhi-prajñā-pūrvaka itareṣām
[Upāya-pratyaya samādhi] when preceded by faith, strength, memory, samādhi, and prajñā (transcendental wisdom) is [attained] by the others (yogīs).

उपाय upāya = to come close, arrive, devote oneself; means, way (from upa + √i, 'to go')
प्रत्यय pratyaya = notion (see I.10)
श्रद्धा śraddhā = faith (from √śrat, 'to assure' + √dhā, 'to put')
वीर्य vīrya = strength, vigor (from √vī, 'to set in motion, arouse, impel' + ya)
स्मृति smṛti = memory; here this is not simply memory, but the constant remembering of the puruṣa, the self (see I.6)
समाधि samādhi = samādhi (from sam + ā + √dhā, 'to put')
प्रज्ञा prajñā = transcendental wisdom (from pra + √jña, 'to know')
पूर्वक pūrvaka = preceding (see pūrva, I.18)
इतर itara = other

तीव्रसंवेगानामासन्नः ॥ १ । २१ ॥
I.21. tīvra-saṃvegānām-āsannaḥ
It is near for the keenly intense.

तीव्र tīvra = keen
संवेग saṃvega = intense (from sam + √vij, 'to move with speed, to be agitated')
आसन्न āsanna = near, in proximity (from ā + √sad, 'to sit')

मृदुमध्याधिमात्रत्वात्ततोऽपि विशेषः ॥ १ । २२ ॥
I.22. mṛdu-madhya-adhimātratvāt-tato'pi viśeṣaḥ
Even here there are differences because it can be mild, medium or very extreme.

मृदु mṛdu = mild, gentle (from √mṛd, 'to to press, squeeze, mingle')
मध्य madhya = medium
अधिमात्र adhimātra = intense, extreme, above measure (from adhi, 'highest' + mātra, 'degree')
ततस् tatas = in that place, there
अपि api = even so
विशेष viśeṣa = difference (from vi + √śiṣ, 'to distinguish')

ईश्वरप्रणिधानाद्वा ॥ १ । २३ ॥
I.23. īśvara-praṇidhānād-vā
Or by devotion to Īśvara.

ईश्वर Īśvara = God, Supreme Being (from √īś, 'Lord' + vara - 'best')
प्रणिधान praṇidhāna = giving, surrender, devotion (from pra + ni + √dha, 'to put')
वा vā = or

क्लेशकर्मविपाकासयैरपरामृष्टः पुरुषविशेष ईश्वरः ॥ १ । २४ ॥
I.24. kleśa-karma-vipāka-āsayair-aparāmṛṣṭaḥ puruṣa-viśeṣa īśvaraḥ
Untouched by kleśas, karma [and its] fruit, [and its] deposits[6]; Īśvara is a special puruṣa.

क्लेश kleśa = cause of pain or afflictions (from √kliś, 'to torment, cause pain; to be afflicted') (see kliṣṭa, I.5)
कर्मन् karman = action (from √kṛ, 'to do')

6 Āśaya - stock or balance of the fruits of previous karma, which lie stored in the mind in the form of mental deposits of merit or demerit, until they ripen in the individual soul's own experience into caste, years and enjoyment.

विपाक vipāka = ripens, bears fruit (from vi + √pac, 'to cook, to ripen')
आशय āśaya - deposit - see footnote (from ā + √śī, 'to lie down to rest')
अपरामृष्ट aparāmṛṣṭa = untouched (from ā + parā + √mṛś, 'to touch')
पुरुष puruṣa = person, Self (see I.16)
विशेष viśeṣa = special (see I.22)
ईश्वर Īśvara = God, Supreme Being (see I.23)

तत्र निरतिशयं सर्वज्ञबीजम् ॥ १ । २५ ॥
I.25. tatra niratiśayaṃ sarva-jña-bījam
There, [in Īśvara], the seed of all knowledge is unsurpassed.

तत्र tatra = there
निरतिशय niratiśaya = ultimate, preeminence, unexcelled, unsurpassed (from nir + ati + √śi, 'to sleep with, lie along or close to, adhere closely to')
सर्व sarva = all
ज्ञ jña = to know (from √jña as in the Latin gnosis)
बीज bīja = seed

पूर्वेषामपि गुरुः कालेनानवच्छेदात् ॥ १ । २६ ॥
I.26. pūrveṣām-api guruḥ kālena-anavacchedāt
Not bound by time, [Īśvara is] also the teacher of the first [yogīs].

पूर्व pūrva = former, earlier (see I.18)
अपि api = also, even so
गुरु guru = heavy, important, teacher (from √gur, 'to raise, lift up, make an effort')
काल kāla = time (see I.14)
अनवच्छेद anavaccheda = unbound, un-separated, indistinct (from an + ava + √chid, 'to cut')

तस्य वाचकः प्रणवः ॥ १ । २७ ॥

I.27. tasya vācakaḥ praṇavaḥ

The word-expressing Him is the praṇava (the mantra - 'a u m').

तस्य tasya = his (here, Him)
वाचक vācaka = (from √vac, 'to speak') literally 'speaking'
प्रणव praṇava = sacred syllable om (from pra + √nu, 'to sound; make a droning, humming sound')

तज्जपस्तदर्थभावनम् ॥ १ । २८ ॥

I.28. taj-japas-tad-artha-bhāvanam

The chanting of it, the contemplation of its objective.

तद् tad = that, it
जपस् japas = repeating in murmuring tone, chanting (from √jap, 'to utter in a low voice'); a known yogic tool for the deepening of meditation and inducing samādhi
अर्थ artha = objective, purpose, aim
भावन bhāvana = contemplation, cultivation (from √bhū, 'to be')

ततः प्रत्यक्चेतनाधिगमोऽप्यन्तरायाभावश्च ॥ १ । २९ ॥

I.29. tataḥ pratyakcetanā-adhigamo'py-antarāya-abhāvaś-ca

Then inward-mindedness is reached, and also the obstacles disappear.

ततस् tatas = there, then, afterwards
प्रत्यक्चेतना pratyak-cetanā = inward-mindedness:
प्रत्यच् pratyac - 'reverse, inward'; चेतन cetana - 'thoughts, awareness, consciousness' (from √cit)
अधिगम adhigama = to attain, acquire, master, reach (from adhi + √gam, 'to go')
अपि api = also, even so (see I.22)
अन्तराय antarāya = obstacle (from antar + √ī, 'to come between, to conceal')
अभाव abhāva = disappear (literally: a, 'not' + √bhū, 'to be')
च ca = and

व्याधिस्त्यानसंशयप्रमादालस्याविरतिभ्रान्तिदर्शनालब्धभूमिकत्वानवस्थितत्वानिचित्तविक्षेपास्तेऽन्तरायाः ॥ १ । ३० ॥

I.30. vyādhi-styāna-saṃśaya-pramāda-ālasya-avirati-bhrānti-darśana-alabdha-bhūmikatva-anavasthitatvāni citta-vikṣepās-te'ntarāyāḥ

Disease, apathy, doubt, carelessness, laziness, incontinence (dissipation), wandering vision, not-reaching the stages [of samādhi] and instability [in them]; these are the distractions of consciousness, these are the obstacles.

व्याधि vyādhi = disorder, disease, sickness (from vi + ā + √dhā, 'to put')

स्त्यान styāna = apathy, denseness, idleness (from √styai, 'to grow dense')

संशय saṃśaya = uncertainty, hesitation, doubt (from sam + √śī, 'to lie down to rest')

प्रमाद् pramāda = carelessness, negligence (from pra + √mad, 'madness, intoxication')

आलस्य ālasya = idleness, sloth, lack of energy

अविरति avirati = incontinence, intemperance, dissipation (from a + vi + √ram, 'to stop')

भ्रान्तिदर्शन bhrānti-darśana = wandering vision:

भ्रान्ति bhrānti = wandering, erring, false (from √bhram, 'to wander about')

दर्शन darśana = sight, vision (from √dṛś, 'to see')

अलब्धभूमिकत्व alabdha-bhūmikatva = not reaching the stages:

अलब्ध alabdha = not-obtaining, not reaching or attaining (from a + √labh, 'obtaining, attaining')

भूमिकत्व bhūmikatva = stage, step, level (from √bhū, 'to be')

अनवस्थितत्व anavasthitatva = unsteadiness, instability (from an + ava + √sthā, 'to stand')

चित्त citta = consciousness (see I.2)

विक्षेप vikṣepa = distraction, disturbance (from vi + √kṣip, 'to throw, to cast')

ते te = they, these (from tad)

अन्तराय antarāya = obstacle (see I.29)

दुःखदौर्मनस्याङ्गमेजयत्वश्वासप्रश्वासा विक्षेपसहभुवः ॥ १ । ३१ ॥

I.31. duḥkha-daurmanasya-aṅgam-ejayatva-śvāsa-praśvāsā vikṣepa-sahabhuvaḥ

Pain, depression, trembling of the limbs, [heavy] inhalation and exhalation accompany the distractions.

दुःख duḥkha = pain, uneasiness, suffering, sorrow (from dus, 'bad' + kha)
दौर्मनस्य daurmanasya = depression, dejection, melancholy (from dus, 'bad' + √man, 'to think')
अङ्ग aṅga = limb (from √aṅg or √am, 'to go')
एजयत्व ejayatva = shaking or trembling (from √ej, 'to stir, move, shake or tremble')
श्वास śvāsa = inhalation (from √śvas, 'to breath, to breath heavily')
प्रश्वास praśvāsa = exhalation (from pra + √śvas)
विक्षेप vikṣepa = distraction, disturbances (see I.30)
सहभुव sahabhuva = accompany (from saha + √bhū, 'to be')

तत्प्रतिषेधार्थमेकतत्त्वाभ्यासः ॥ १ । ३२ ॥

I.32. tat-pratiṣedha-artham-eka-tattva-abhyāsaḥ

The practice on one principle with the purpose of checking these.

तद् tad = these; refer to the distractions and the physical suffering that accompanies them
प्रतिषेध pratiṣedha = to check, keep back, ward off (from prati + √sidh, 'to drive away, ward off')
अर्थ artha = object, purpose, aim (see I.28)
एकतत्त्व eka tattva[7]:
एक eka = one

7 eka-tattva: In Sāṃkhya Philosophy there are 25 tattvas: the five tanmātras, the five mahā-bhūtas, the 11 organs including manas, and lastly puruṣa. When the sūtra states eka-tattva it could be that it telling us to choose one of the 25 tattvas. But perhaps it is more likely that eka-tattva implies the puruṣa, the final reality.

तत्त्व tattva = true principle, truth, reality
अभ्यास abhyāsa = practice (see I.12)

मैत्रीकरुणामुदितोपेक्षाणां सुखदुःखपुण्यापुण्यविषयाणां भावनातश्चित्तप्रसादनम् ॥ १ । ३३ ॥
I.33. maitrī-karuṇā-muditā-upekṣāṇāṃ sukha-duḥkha-puṇya-apuṇya-viṣayāṇāṃ bhāvanātaś-citta-prasādanam
Cultivating friendliness, kindness, gladness, and equanimity (wide-eyes) towards objects of joy, suffering, merit, or demerit [bring about] calm clarity of the consciousness.[8]

मैत्री maitrī = friendliness (from mitra-friend)
करुणा karuṇā = kindness, compassion (from √kṛ, 'to do')
मुदिता muditā = gladness (from √mud, 'to rejoice')
उपेक्षा upekṣā = equanimity, wide eyes (from upa + √īkṣ, 'to see')
सुख sukha = pleasant, joyful (from su, 'good' + kha)
दुःख duḥkha = pain, suffering, sorrow (see I.31)
पुण्य puṇya = merit (from √puṇ, 'to do good')
अपुण्य apuṇya = demerit (from a + √puṇ)
विषय viṣaya = object (see I.11)
भावनातस् bhāvanātas = cultivating (from √bhū, 'to be')
चित्त citta = consciousness (see I.2)
प्रसादन prasādana = clearing, calming (from pra + √sad, 'to sit')

प्रच्छर्दनविधारणाभ्यां वा प्राणस्य ॥ १ । ३४ ॥
I.34. pracchardana-vidhāraṇābhyāṃ vā prāṇasya
Or by exhalation and retention of prāṇa.

प्रच्छर्दन pracchardana = exhalation, expulsion (from pra + √chrid, 'to vomit')
विधारण vidhāraṇa = retention (from vi + √dhā, 'to put')
वा vā = or
प्राण prāṇa = breath

8 This sūtra is parallel to the Buddhist notion on the basic attitude towards these four primal situations we encounter in everyday life.

विषयवती वा प्रवृत्तिरुत्पन्ना मनसः स्थितिनिबन्धनी ॥ १ । ३५ ॥

I.35. viṣaya-vatī vā pravṛttir-utpannā manasaḥ sthiti-nibandhanī

Or an activity arises towards an object which binds the mind to stability.

विषय viṣaya = object (see I.11)
वती vatī = 'having'
वा vā = or
प्रवृत्ति pravṛtti = activity (from pra + √vṛt, 'to turn, to whirl')
उत्पन्न utpanna = arisen (from ud, + √pad, 'to fall')
मनस् manas = mind (from √man, 'to think')
स्थिति sthiti = stability (see I.13)
निबन्धनिन् nibandhanin = binds (from ni + √bandh, 'to bind')

विशोका वा ज्योतिष्मती ॥ १ । ३६ ॥

I.36. viśokā vā jyotiṣmatī

Or by sorrowless and illuminating [activity].

विशोक viśoka = sorrowless (from vi + √śuc, 'to burn')
वा vā = or
ज्योतिष्मती jyotiṣ-matī = illuminating: jyotis, 'light' (from √jyut, 'to shine' + mant, 'consisting of')

वीतरागविषयं वा चित्तम् ॥ १ । ३७ ॥

I.37. vīta-rāga-viṣayaṃ vā cittam

Or citta (consciousness) has objects free of attachment.

वीत vīta = gone away, lost, without (from √vī, 'to be defused, scattered; to be lost; to perish)
राग rāga = attachment, color, red color, any feeling of passion, vehement desire (from √raj, 'to be excited')
विषय viṣaya = object (see I.11)
वा vā = or
चित्त citta = mind, consciousness (see I.2)

स्वप्ननिद्राज्ञानालम्बनं वा ॥ १ । ३८ ॥

I.38. svapna-nidrā-jñāna-ālambanaṃ vā

Or [citta is] supported by knowledge [that comes] in dream or sleep.

स्वप्न svapna = sleep, dream (from √svap, 'to sleep; to lie down, recline')
निद्रा nidrā = sleep (see I.6)
ज्ञान jñāna = knowledge (see I.8)
आलम्बन ālambana = support (see I.10)
वा vā = or

यथाभिमतध्यानाद्वा ॥ १ । ३९ ॥

I.39. yathā-abhimata-dhyānād-vā

Or by meditation as desired.

यथा yathā = as
अभिमत abhimata = longed for, wished, desired (from abhi + √man, 'to think')
ध्याना dhyānā = meditation, thought, reflection (from √dhyai, 'to think of, imagine, contemplate, meditate on')
वा vā = or

परमाणुपरममहत्त्वान्तोऽस्य वशीकारः ॥ १ । ४० ॥

I.40. parama-aṇu-parama-mahattva-anto'sya vaśīkāraḥ

His mastery [spreads] from the most minute to the most immense.

परम parama = primary, most excellent, extreme (from √pṛ, 'to surpass, excel')
अणु aṇu = fine, minute, atom
महत्त्व mahattva = great size, extent, magnitude (from √mah, 'to magnify, esteem highly')
अन्त anta = end, limit (here: from... to)
अस्य asya = his
वशीकार vaśīkāra = mastery (see I.15)

क्षीणवृत्तेरभिजातस्येव मणेर्ग्रहीतृग्रहणग्राह्येषु तत्स्थतदञ्जनता समापत्तिः ॥ १ । ४१ ॥

I.41. kṣīṇa-vṛtter-abhijātasya-iva maṇer-grahītṛ-grahaṇa-grāhyeṣu tat-stha-tad-añjanatā samāpattiḥ

When the vṛttis have decreased, [the citta is] transparent like a jewel; it abides in, [and] is colored by the 'grasper, the grasping and the grasped'. This is Samāpatti.[9]

क्षीण kṣīṇa = decreased, dwindled (from √kṣi, 'to decrease')
वृत्ति vṛtti = activity, movement, function, wave (see I.2)
अभिजात abhijāta = precious, transparent (from abhi + √jan, 'to beget')
इव iva = like, as if, as it were
मणि maṇi = jewel
ग्रहीतृ grahītṛ = grasper, perceiver (from √grah, 'to grasp'+ tṛ)
ग्रहण grahaṇa = grasping, perceiving
ग्राह्य grāhya = grasped
तद् tad = that
स्थ stha = abiding (from √sthā, 'to stand')
अञ्जनता añjanatā = colored, anointed (from √añj, 'to color' + ana + tā)
समापत्ति samāpatti = (from sam - 'with, together with' + ā - 'near to, towards' + √pat, 'to fall') literally 'coming together', another name for samādhi

तत्र शब्दार्थज्ञानविकल्पैः संकीर्णा सवितर्का समापत्तिः ॥ १ । ४२ ॥

I.42. tatra śabda-artha-jñāna-vikalpaiḥ saṃkīrṇā savitarkā samāpattiḥ

Samāpatti with thought [occurs] where word, meaning, knowledge and imagination intermingle.

तत्र tatra = where
शब्द śabda = sound, word (see I.9)
अर्थ artha = objective, purpose, aim (see I.28)
ज्ञान jñāna = knowledge (see I.8)

9 The question would then be is the citta coloured simultaneously by the grasper, the grasping and the grasped, or by each of them seperately.

विकल्प vikalpa = imagination, mental construction (see I.9)
संकीर्ण saṃkīrṇa = mixed, intermingled (from sam + √kṝ, 'to pour out, scatter')
सवितर्क savitarka = with thought (from sa, 'with' + vitarka, 'thought, supposition'; (see I.17)
समापत्ति samāpatti (see I.41)

स्मृतिपरिशुद्धौ स्वरुपशून्येवार्थमात्रनिर्भासा निर्वितर्का ॥ १ । ४३ ॥
I.43. smṛti-pariśuddhau sva-rūpa-śūnya-iva-artha-mātra-nirbhāsā nirvitarkā
[Samāpatti] without thought [occurs where] memory is purified and is as if empty of its own form, and only the object shines forth.

स्मृति smṛti = memory (see I.6)
परिशुद्धि pariśuddhi = purified (from pari + √śudh, 'to be cleansed, purified')
स्वरूप sva-rūpa = own form (see I.3)
शून्य śūnya = empty, void (see I.9)
इव iva = as it were, as if
अर्थ artha = objective, purpose, aim (see I.28)
मात्र mātra = only, merely, just
निर्भास nirbhāsa = shining forth, illuminating, making manifest (from nir + √bhās, 'to shine, be bright')
निर्वितर्क nirvitarka = without thought (from nir, 'without' + vitarka, 'thought, supposition') (see I.17)

एतयैव सविचारा निर्विचारा च सूक्ष्मविषया व्याख्याता ॥ १ । ४४ ॥
I.44. etayā-eva savicārā nirvicārā ca sūkṣma-viṣayā vyākhyātā
By this [samāpatti] with reflection and without reflection are explained. They have subtle objects.

एतया etayā = by this (from tad, 'that')
एव eva = also
सविचार savicāra = with reflection (from sa, 'with' + vicāra, 'reflection, deliberation, consideration'; see I.17)

निर्विचार nirvicāra = without reflection (from nir, 'without' + vicāra)
च ca = and
सूक्ष्म sūkṣma = subtle, minute, small
विषय viṣaya = object (see I.11)
व्याख्यात vyākhyāta = explained (from vi + ā + √khyā, 'to know')

सूक्ष्मविषयत्वं चालिङ्गपर्यवसानम् ॥ १ । ४५ ॥
I.45. sūkṣma-viṣayatvaṃ ca-aliṅga-paryavasānam
And the subtle object ends in the aliṅga (unmarked).

सूक्ष्म sūkṣma = subtle (see I.44)
विषय viṣaya = object (see I.11)
च ca = and
अलिङ्ग aliṅga = without mark, without sign (from a + liṅg, 'mark, sign')
पर्यवसान paryavasāna = end, termination, conclusion (from pari + ava + √so, 'to finish')

ता एव सबीजः समाधिः ॥ १ । ४६ ॥
I.46. tā eva sabījaḥ samādhiḥ
Even these are samādhi with seed.

ताः tāḥ = these (from tad)
एव eva = even
सबीज sabīja = with seed (sa + bīja, 'seed')
समाधि samādhi see I.20

निर्विचारवैशारद्येऽध्यात्मप्रसादः ॥ १ । ४७ ॥
I.47. nirvicāra-vaiśāradye'dhyātma-prasādaḥ
Lucidity in [Samāpatti] without reflection - calm clarity in oneself.

निर्विचार nirvicāra = without reflection (see I.44)
वैशारद्य vaiśāradya = lucidity, clearness of intellect, skill (from vi + śārada, 'mature')
अध्यात्मन् adhyātman = oneself (from adhi + ātma, self)
प्रसाद prasāda = calmness, clarity (see I.33)

ऋतंभरा तत्र प्रज्ञा ॥ १ । ४८ ॥

I.48. ṛtaṃ-bharā tatra prajñā

There prajñā (transcendental knowledge) is truth-bearing.

ऋत ṛta = order, the right

भरा bharā = bearing (from √bhṛ, 'to bear')

तत्र tatra = there (see I.13)

प्रज्ञा prajñā = transcendental wisdom (see I.20)

श्रुतानुमानप्रज्ञाभ्यामन्यविषया विशेषार्थत्वात् ॥ १ । ४९ ॥

I.49. śruta-anumāna-prajñābhyām-anya-viṣayā viśeṣa-arthatvāt

The object is different from that arising from prajñā [reached] by tradition and inference, because of its specific purpose-ness.

श्रुत śruta = heard, tradition (from √śru, 'to hear')

अनुमान anumāna = inference (see I.7)

प्रज्ञा prajñā = transcendental wisdom (see I.20)

अन्य anya = other

विषय viṣaya = object (see I.11)

विशेष viśeṣa = difference, specific (see I.22)

अर्थत्व arthatva = 'purpose-ness', objective (from artha + tva)

तज्जः संस्कारोऽन्यसंस्कारप्रतिबन्धी ॥ १ । ५० ॥

I.50. taj-jaḥ saṃskāro'nya-saṃskāra-pratibandhī

The saṃskāra born from that impedes the other saṃskāras.

तद् tad = that

ज ja = born (from √jan, 'to beget')

संस्कार saṃskāra = [mental] imprint (see footnote, I.18)

अन्य anya = other

प्रतिबन्धिन् pratibandhin = to oppose, to obstruct, to impede (from prati + √bandh, 'to bind')

तस्यापि निरोधे सर्वनिरोधान्निर्बीजः समाधिः ॥ १ । ५१ ॥

I.51. tasya-api nirodhe sarva-nirodhān-nirbījaḥ samādhiḥ

[When] also this is restrained, all is restrained. [This] is samādhi without seed.

तस्य tasya = of this
अपि api = also, even so
निरोध nirodha = restrained (see I.2)
सर्व sarva = all
निर्बीज nirbīja = without seed (from nir [nis] + bīja, 'seed')
समाधि samādhi - see I.20

साधनपादः Chapter II - Sādhana Pāda

साधन sādhana = path, means
पाद् pāda = chapter

तपः स्वाध्यायेश्वरप्रणिधानानि क्रियायोगः ॥ २ । १ ॥
II.1. tapaḥ svādhyāya-īśvara-praṇidhānāni kriyā-yogaḥ
Kriyā Yoga is made of Tapas[10] (heating disciplines), self-study and devotion to Īśvara.

तपस् tapas - see footnote (from the root √tap, 'to heat')
स्वाध्याय svādhyāya = (from sva - 'self' + adhi + ā - 'near to, towards' + √i, 'to go') - literally to go into oneself, therefore self-study. Usually the classical commentators explain this as study of the scriptures.
ईश्वर Īśvara = God, Supreme Being (from √īś, 'Lord' + vara - 'best') (see I.23)
प्रणिधान praṇidhāna = giving, surrender, devotion (from pra + ni + √dha, 'to put') (see I.23)
क्रिया kriyā = action (from √kṛ, 'to do')
योग yoga = from √yuj, 'to yoke, to join together' (see I.1)

10 *Tapas* - a well-known, technical term for yogic practices that heat the mental-physical system of the yogi. Through the heat, the yogi is purified and also attains powers. In Indian mythology there are many tales of Yogins who through many years of tapas, (usually sitting in meditation), attained spiritual heights.

समाधिभावनार्थः क्लेशतनूकरणार्थश्च ॥ २ । २ ॥

II.2. samādhi-bhāvana-arthaḥ kleśa-tanū-karaṇa-arthaś-ca

With the purpose of cultivating Samādhi and with the purpose of making thin the Kleśas.

समाधि samādhi = a kind of trance or high state of consciousness (from sam + ā + √dhā, 'to put') (see I.20)
भावन bhāvana = cultivating (from √bhū, 'to be')
अर्थ artha = objective, purpose (see I.28)
क्लेश kleśa = cause of pain or afflictions (from √kliś, 'to torment, cause pain; to be afflicted) (see I.24)
तनू tanū = fine, thin
करण karaṇa = doing, making, effecting, causing (from √kṛ, 'to do')
च ca = and[11]

अविद्यास्मितारागद्वेषाभिनिवेशाः पञ्चक्लेशाः ॥ २ । ३ ॥

II.3. avidyā-asmitā-rāga-dveṣa-abhiniveśāḥ pañca-kleśāḥ[12]

The five kleśas are not-knowing, 'I am'ness, attachment or desire, aversion or hatred, and the will-to-live (fear-of-death).

अविद्या avidyā = not-knowing, ignorance (from a - 'not' + √vid, 'to know')
अस्मिता asmitā = literally 'I am'ness (see I.17)
राग rāga = attachment, color, red color, any feeling of passion,

11 Kriyā yoga has two main objectives. One is to cultivate Samādhi. But Samādhi, which is the essence of yoga, cannot be properly integrated into our mental-physical frame if the Kleśas (the causes of pain) are not dealt with. Because of this, kriyā-yoga by the three means - tapas, self study and devotion to Iśvara - aims at two broad objectives. The first is positive, creating an environment for Samādhi. The second is negating, to thin out the negative influence of the Kleśas.

12 In some editions, this sūtra is written without the word 'five':
अविद्यास्मितारागद्वेषाभिनिवेशाः क्लेशाः ।
avidyā-asmitā-rāga-dveṣa-abhiniveśāḥ kleśāḥ

vehement desire (from √raj, 'to be excited') (see I.37)
द्वेष dveṣa = aversion, hatred, dislike (from √dviṣ, 'to hate')
अभिनिवेष abhiniveśa = the will-to-live, fear-of-death (from abhi + ni + √viś, 'to dwell, to be intent, to adhere')
पञ्च pañca = five
क्लेश kleśa = cause of pain or afflictions (see II.2)

अविद्या क्षेत्रमुत्तरेषां प्रसुप्ततनुविच्छिन्नोदाराणाम् ॥ २ । ४ ॥
II.4. avidyā kṣetram-uttareṣāṃ prasupta-tanu-vicchinnodārāṇām
Avidyā [not-knowing] is the field of the others whether they be dormant, thinned out, interrupted or aroused.

अविद्या avidyā = not-knowing (see II.3)
क्षेत्र kṣetra = field
उत्तर uttara = others
प्रसुप्त prasupta = dormant (from pra + √svap, 'to sleep')
तनु tanu = thinned out, weakened (from √tan, 'to stretch', like uttānāsana)
विच्छिन्न vicchinna = cut off, interrupted, alternated (from vi + √chid, 'to cut')
उदार udāra = aroused (from ud + √ṛ, 'to move')

अनित्याशुचिदुःखानात्मसु नित्यशुचिसुखात्मख्यातिरविद्या ॥ २ । ५ ॥
II.5. anitya-aśuci-duḥkha-anātmasu nitya-śuci-sukha-ātma-khyātir-avidyā
Avidyā is envisioning the permanent, the pure, the joyful and the ātman in what is impermanent, impure, painful and not the ātman.

नित्य nitya = permanent, eternal (from ni - 'down, back, in, into, within' + tya - 'not permanent')
अनित्य anitya = impermanent (from a - 'not' + nitya)
शुचि śuci = pure (from √śuc, 'to purify')
अशुचि aśuci = impure (from a - 'not' + śuci)
आत्मन् ātman = self spirit, essence
अनात्मन् anātman = not-ātman (from an + ātman)

दुःख duḥkha = pain, suffering, sorrow (see I.31)
सुख sukha = pleasant, joyful (see I.33)
ख्याति khyāti = to perceive, to envision (from √khyā, 'to know') (see I.16)
अविद्या avidyā = ignorance (see II.3)

दृग्दर्शनशक्त्योरेकात्मतेवास्मिता ॥ २ । ६ ॥
II.6. dṛg-darśana-śaktyor-eka-ātmateva-asmitā
Asmitā [occurs] when the powers of seeing and of the seer are as if a single self.

दृश् dṛś = seer (from √dṛś, 'to see')
दर्शन darśana = seeing, seen (see I.30)
शक्ति śakti = power (from √śak, 'to be able to')
एक eka = one, single
आत्मता ātmatā = 'self'ness
इव iva = as it were
अस्मिता asmitā = literally - 'I am'ness (see II.3)

सुखानुशयी रागः ॥ २ । ७ ॥
II.7. sukha-anuśayī rāgaḥ
Attachment is that which follows pleasure.

सुख sukha = pleasure, pleasant, joyousness (see II.5) (see I.33)
अनुशयिन् anuśayin = follows, connected as with a consequence (from anu - near + √śī, 'to sleep with, lie along, adhere closely to')
राग rāga = attachment, color, red color, any feeling of passion, vehement desire (see II.3)

दुःखानुशयी द्वेषः ॥ २ । ८ ॥
II.8. duḥkha-anuśayī dveṣaḥ
Aversion is that which follows sorrow.

दुःख duḥkha = pain, suffering, sorrow (see I.31)
अनुशयिन् anuśayin = follows (see II.7)
द्वेष dveṣa = aversion, hatred, dislike (see II.3)

स्वरसवाही विदुषोऽपि तथारूढोऽभिनिवेशः ॥ २ । ९ ॥

II.9. sva-rasa-vāhī viduṣo'pi tathā-rūḍho'bhiniveśaḥ[13]

The will-to-live [life instinct], flowing by its own potency, is rooted thus even in the wise ones.

स्व sva = own
रस rasa = potency (from √ras, 'to taste')
वाहिन् vāhin = flowing (from √vah, 'to flow')
विद्वांस् vidvāṃs = knowing one, wise (from √vid, 'to know')
अपि api = also, even
तथा tathā = thus (see footnote below)
रूढ rūḍha = rooted (from √ruh, 'to grow')
अभिनिवेश abhiniveśa = the will-to-live, fear-of-death (see II.3)

ते प्रतिप्रसवहेयाः सूक्ष्माः ॥ २ । १० ॥

II.10. te pratiprasava-heyāḥ sūkṣmāḥ

These [in their] subtle [form] are overcome by involution.

ते te = these
प्रतिप्रसव pratiprasava = re-emergence into the origin or involution (from prati + pra + √sū, 'to set in motion')
हेय heya = overcome (from √hā, 'to leave, abandon')
सूक्ष्म sūkṣma = subtle (see I.44)

ध्यानहेयास्तद्वृत्तयः ॥ २ । ११ ॥

II.11. dhyāna-heyās-tad-vṛttayaḥ

Their vṛttis are overcome by meditation.

ध्यान dhyāna = meditation (see I.39)
हेय heya = overcome (see II.10)
तद् tad = that, here: their

13 In some editions, this sūtra is written with the word 'samā' (same) instead of 'tathā' (thus): तथारूढः tathā-rūḍhaḥ (rooted thus) समारूढः samā-rūḍhaḥ (rooted same)

वृत्ति vṛtti = activity, movement, function, wave (from √vṛt, 'to turn, to whirl') (see I.2)

क्लेशमूलः कर्माशयो दृष्टादृष्टजन्मवेदनीयः ॥ २ । १२ ॥

II.12. kleśa-mūlaḥ karma-āśayo dṛṣṭa-adṛṣṭa-janma-vedanīyaḥ

The kleśas are the root of the karma-deposit[14] and this can be experienced in seen and unseen births.

क्लेश kleśa = cause of pain or afflictions (see I.24)
मूल mūla = root
कर्मन् karman = action (from √kṛ, 'to do') (see I.24)
आशय āśaya - see footnote (from ā + √śī, 'to lie down to rest') (see I.24)
दृष्ट dṛṣṭa = seen (from √dṛś, 'to see') (see I.15)
अदृष्ट adṛṣṭa = unseen
जन्मन् janman = birth, origin, life (from √jan, 'to beget')
वेदनीय vedanīya = experienced, known (from √vid, 'to know')

सति मूले तद्विपाको जात्यायुर्भोगाः ॥ २ । १३ ॥

II.13. sati mūle tad-vipāko jāty-āyur-bhogāḥ

So long as the root exists, it ripens into birth, life and bhoga.

सति sati = being, existing (from √as, 'to be')
मूल mūla = root
तद् tad = that, it
विपाक vipāka = ripens, bears fruit (see I.24)
जाति jāti = birth (from √jan, 'to beget')
आयुस् āyus = life (from ā + √i, 'to go')
भोग bhoga = experience, enjoyment (from √bhuj, 'to enjoy')

14 **Āśaya** - stock or balance of the fruits of previous karma, which lie stored in the mind in the form of mental deposits of merit or demerit, until they ripen in the individual soul's own experience into caste, years and enjoyment.

ते ह्लादपरितापफलाः पुण्यापुण्यहेतुत्वात् ॥ २ । १४ ॥

II.14. te hlāda-paritāpa-phalāḥ puṇya-apuṇya-hetutvāt

The fruits of these are delight or anguish caused by merit or demerit.

ते te = they, these
ह्लाद hlāda = delight (from √hlād, 'to rejoice')
परिताप paritāpa = anguish (from pari + √tāp, 'to be hot, anxious, anguished')
फल phala = fruit
पुण्य puṇya = merit (from √puṇ, 'to do good') (see I.33)
अपुण्य apuṇya = demerit (see I.33)
हेतुत्व hetutva = 'causality', caused (from hetu, see II.17)

परिणामतापसंस्कारदुःखैर्गुणवृत्तिविरोधच्च दुःखमेव सर्वं विवेकिनः ॥ २ । १५ ॥

II.15. pariṇāma-tāpa-saṃskāra-duḥkhair-guṇa-vṛtti-virodhāc-ca duḥkham-eva sarvaṃ vivekinaḥ

Due to the sorrow in the process of change, in anxiety, in the saṃskāras and also due to the conflict of fluctuating guṇas - to him who discerns everything is suffering.

परिणाम pariṇāma = change (from pari + √nam, 'to bend, to turn aside; to change, to be transformed')
ताप tāpa = anxiety, anguish (see paritāpa, II.14)
संस्कार saṃskāra = [mental] imprint (see footnote, I.18)
दुःख duḥkha = pain, suffering, sorrow (see I.31)
गुण guṇa = see footnote I.16
वृत्ति vṛtti = activity, movement, function, wave (see I.2)
विरोध virodha = opposition, conflict (from vi + √rudh, 'to be impeded, checked back, withheld')
च ca = and
एव eva = also
सर्व sarva = all
विवेकिन् vivekin = discerner, one who discerns (from vi + √vic, 'to sift, to separate from; to discern')

हेयं दुःखमनागतम् ॥ २ । १६ ॥
II.16. heyaṃ duḥkham-anāgatam
The suffering, which is yet to come, is to be avoided.

हेय heya = to be left, overcome, avoided, quitted or abandoned (see II.10)
दुःख duḥkha = pain, suffering, sorrow (see I.31)
अनागत anāgata = not come, not arrived; the future (from an + ā + √gam, 'to go')

द्रष्टृदृश्ययोः संयोगो हेयहेतुः ॥ २ । १७ ॥
II.17. draṣṭṛ-dṛśyayoḥ saṃyogo heya overcome, avoided
The connection of the Seer with the seen is the cause of that which is to be avoided.

द्रष्टृ draṣṭṛ = the see'er (see I.3)
दृश्य dṛśya = the seen (from √dṛś, 'to see')
संयोग saṃyoga = conjunction, combination, connection, union (from sam + √yuj, 'to yoke, to join together')
हेय heya = avoidance (see II.10)
हेतु hetu = impulse, motive, cause (from √hi, 'to set in motion, to impel')

प्रकाशक्रियास्थितिशीलं भूतेन्द्रियात्मकं भोगापवर्गार्थं दृश्यम् ॥ २ । १८ ॥
II.18. prakāśa-kriyā-sthiti-śīlaṃ bhuta-indriya-ātmakaṃ bhoga-apavarga-arthaṃ dṛśyam
The seen has the tendency of brightness, action, and stability - it is embodied in the elements and the senses and its purpose is bhoga- experience and apavarga- completion.

प्रकाश prakāśa = brightness (from pra + √kāś, 'to be visible; to shine')
क्रिया kriyā = action (see II.1)
स्थिति sthiti = standing, remaining, steadiness, stability (see I.13)
शील śīla = disposition, nature, tendency, character

भूत bhūta = element (from √bhū, 'to be')
इन्द्रिय indriya = sense, faculty of sense, sense-organ (from indra + ya)
आत्मक ātmaka = having the nature of, tendency (from ātman + ka)
भोग bhoga = experience, enjoyment (see note, II.13)
अपवर्ग apavarga = completion, end, the emancipation of the soul from bodily existence (from apa + √vṛj, 'to bend, to turn, to give up, renounce')
अर्थ artha = aim, object, purpose (see I.28)
दृश्य dṛśya = the seen (see II.17)

विशेषाविशेषलिङ्गमात्रालिङ्गानि गुणपर्वाणि ॥ २ । १९ ॥
II.19. viśeṣa-aviśeṣa-liṅga-mātra-aliṅgāni guṇa-parvāṇi
The divisions of the guṇas are particular, not particular, with sign and without sign.

विशेष viśeṣa = distinct, particular (see I.22)
अविशेष aviśeṣa = not distinct, unparticular
लिङ्ग liṅga = sign, mark
अलिङ्ग aliṅga = without sign (see I.45)
मात्र mātra = merely, scarcely, just, only
गुण guṇa = (see footnote I.16)
पर्वन् parvan = limb, member; division, section

द्रष्टा दृशिमात्रः शुद्धोऽपि प्रत्ययानुपश्यः ॥ २ । २० ॥
II.20. draṣṭā dṛśi-mātraḥ śuddho'pi pratyaya-anupaśyaḥ
The Seer who is but seeing, although pure, perceives notions.

द्रष्टृ draṣṭṛ = 'see'er (see I.3)
दृशि dṛśi = seeing (from √dṛś, 'to see')
मात्र mātra = merely, scarcely, just, only (here: but)
शुद्ध śuddha = pure (from √śudh, 'to be cleansed, purified')
अपि api = also, even so, although
प्रत्यय pratyaya = notion (see I.10)
अनुपश्य anupaśya = perceives (from anu + √paś, 'to see, observe, perceive')

तदर्थ एव दृश्यस्यात्मा ॥ २ । २१ ॥
II.21. tad-artha eva dṛśyasya-ātmā
The essence of the seen is for that purpose only.
तद् tad = that
अर्थ artha = object, purpose (see I.28)
एव eva = only
दृश्य dṛśya = (the) seen (see II.17)
आत्मन् ātman = self, spirit, essence (see II.5)

कृतार्थं प्रति नष्टमप्यनष्टं तदन्यसाधारणत्वात् ॥ २ । २२ ॥
II.22. kṛta-arthaṃ prati naṣṭam-apy-anaṣṭaṃ tad-anya-sādhāraṇatvāt
Although for him whose purpose is fulfilled it disappears, it still hasn't disappeared for others since it is (the) common experience.

कृत kṛta = done, made, accomplished, fulfilled (from √kṛ, 'to do')
अर्थ artha = objective, purpose (see I.28)
प्रति prati = with regard to, for (near to, in the direction of)
नष्ट naṣṭa = disappeared (from √naś, 'to be lost, perish, disappear')
अनष्ट anaṣṭa = not-disappeared (see above)
अपि api = even so, still
तद् tad = it
अन्य anya = other
साधारणत्व sādhāraṇatva = common experience (from sa + ā + √dhṛ, 'to hold, maintain, preserve' + na + tva)

स्वस्वामिशक्त्योः स्वरूपोपलब्धिहेतुः संयोगः ॥ २ । २३ ॥
II.23. sva-svāmi-śaktyoḥ sva-rūpa-upalabdhi-hetuḥ saṃyogaḥ
Saṃyoga is the cause of 'catching sight' of the true form of the powers of the owner and the owned.

स्व sva = owned
स्वामिन् svāmin = owner, master (from sva)
शक्ति śakti = power (see II.6)
स्वरूप sva-rūpa = own form, true form (see I.3)
उपलब्धि upalabdhi = obtainment, observation, 'catching sight'

(from upa + √labh, 'to take, catch sight of, obtain')
हेतु hetu = impulse, motive, cause (see II.17)
संयोग saṃyoga = conjunction, combination, connection (see II.17)

तस्य हेतुरविद्या ॥ २ । २४ ॥
II.24. tasya hetur-avidyā
Its [saṃyoga] cause is avidyā - not-knowing.

तस्य tasya = its, his
हेतु hetu = impulse, motive, cause (see II.17)
अविद्या avidyā = not-knowing, ignorance (see II.3)

तदभावात् संयोगाभावो हानं तद्दृशेः कैवल्यम् ॥ २ । २५ ॥
II.25. tad-abhāvāt saṃyoga-abhāvo hānaṃ tad-dṛśeḥ kaivalyam
When this [avidyā] does not exist, saṃyoga does not exist; this is relinquishing - the Aloneness[15] of seeing.

तद् tad = that, this
अभाव abhāva = non-becoming (see I.10)
संयोग saṃyoga = conjunction, combination, connection, association (see II.17)
हान hāna = the act of abandoning, relinquishing, giving up, escaping (from √hā, 'to leave, abandon')
दृशि dṛśi = seeing (see II.20)
कैवल्य kaivalya = aloneness (from kevala, 'alone') [see footnote]

15 ***Kaivalya*** relates to an exclusive and continual vision of the self. At the end of a spiritual journey, from which there is no turning back, a reality of exclusive vision is formed. This is the 'Aloneness' of the Self.

विवेकख्यातिरविप्लवा हानोपायः ॥ २ । २६ ॥
II.26. viveka-khyātir-aviplavā hāna-upāyaḥ
The means to relinquishing - by the unwavering vision (view) of discernment.

विवेक viveka = discernment (see II.15)
ख्याति khyāti = to perceive, to have vision (see I.16)
अविप्लव aviplava = (avipluta) unwavering, undeviating, steadily observing (from avi + √plu, 'to float, to swim; to pass away')
हान hāna = abandoning, relinquishing, giving up, escaping (see II.25)
उपाय upāya = to arrive, devote oneself; means, way (see I.20)

तस्य सप्तधा प्रान्तभूमिः प्रज्ञा ॥ २ । २७ ॥
II.27. tasya saptadhā prānta-bhūmiḥ prajñā
For him on the last step there is prajña sevenfold.

तस्य tasya = from tad, here: for him
सप्तध saptadha = sevenfold (from sapta, 'seven' + dha)
प्रान्त prānta = last (from pra + anta, 'end, limit')
भूमि bhūmi = step, stage; earth (see I.14)
प्रज्ञा prajñā = transcendental wisdom (see I.20)

योगाङ्गानुष्ठानादशुद्धिक्षये ज्ञानदीप्तिराविवेकख्यातेः ॥ २ । २८ ॥
II.28. yoga-aṅga-anuṣṭhānād-aśuddhi-kṣaye jñāna-dīptir-ā-viveka-khyāteḥ
By performing the 'limbs' of yoga, the impurities are diminished [and] the light of knowledge [reaches] unto the vision of discernment.

योग yoga - see I.1
अङ्ग aṅga = limb, member, component (see I.31)
अनुष्ठान anuṣṭhāna = carrying out, undertaking, performance, religious practice (from anu + √sthā, 'to stand')
अशुद्धि aśuddhi = impurity (from a + √śudh, 'to be cleansed, purified')
क्षय kṣaya = destruction, reduction (from √kṣi, 'to destroy, to be diminished')

ज्ञान jñāna = knowledge (see I.8)
दीप्ति dīpti = brightness, light, splendor, beauty (from √dip, 'to blaze, flare, shine, illuminate')
आ ā = unto, until, as far as
विवेक viveka = discernment (see II.15)
ख्याति khyāti = to perceive, to have vision (see I.16)

यमनियमासनप्राणायामप्रत्याहारधारणाध्यानसमाधयोऽष्टावङ्गानि ॥ २ । २९ ॥
II.29. yama-niyama-āsana-prāṇāyāma-pratyāhāra-dhāraṇā-dhyāna-samādhayo' ṣṭāv-aṅgāni
The eight 'limbs' are: outer directives, inner directives, posture, breath-control, sense-withdrawal, concentration, meditation and samādhi.

यम yama = outer directives (from √yam, 'to hold or keep in, to restrain')
नियम niyama = inner directives (from ni + √yam)
आसन āsana = posture (from √ās, 'to sit')
प्राणायाम prāṇāyāma = breath-control (from prāṇa + ā + √yam 'to hold or keep in, restrain, control')
प्रत्याहार pratyāhāra = sense-withdrawal (from prati, + ā + √hṛ, 'to withhold, to retain')
धारणा dhāraṇā = concentration (from dhṛ, 'to hold, maintain, preserve)
ध्यान dhyāna = meditation, thought, reflection (see I.39)
समाधि samādhi = (see I.20)
अष्ट aṣṭa = eight
अङ्ग aṅga = limb (see I.31)

अहिंसासत्यास्तेयब्रह्मचर्यापरिग्रहा यमाः ॥ २ । ३० ॥

II.30. ahiṃsā-satya-asteya-brahmacarya-aparigrahā yamāḥ

The yamas (outer directives) are non-harming, truthfulness, non-stealing, continence and non-greed.

अहिंसा ahiṃsā = non-harming (from a - 'not' + √han, 'to hurt, wound')
सत्य satya = truth, truthfulness (from √as, 'to be')
अस्तेय asteya = non-stealing (from a - 'not' + √stai, 'to steal')
ब्रह्मचर्य brahmacarya = continence (from brahma + √car, 'to move')
अपरिग्रह aparigraha = non-greed (from a - 'not' + pari + √grah, 'to grasp')
यम yama = outer directive (see II.29)

जातिदेशकालसमयानवच्छिन्नाः सार्वभौमा महाव्रतम् ॥ २ । ३१ ॥

II.31. jāti-deśa-kāla-samaya-anavacchinnāḥ sārva-bhaumā mahā-vratam

This is the great universal vow unconditioned by birth, place, time and circumstance.

जाति jāti = birth (see II.13)
देश deśa = place (from √diś, 'to point out')
काल kāla = time (see I.14)
समय samaya = coming together, meeting, occasion, juncture, circumstance (from sam + √i, 'to go')
अनवच्छिन्न anavacchinna = 'unseparated', unconditioned (from an + ava + √chid, 'to cut')
सर्व sarva = all
भौम bhauma = stage, layer, level, strata
महन्त् mahant = great
व्रत vrata = vow (from √vṛ, 'to choose')

शौचसंतोषतपःस्वाध्यायेश्वरप्रणिधानानि नियमाः ॥ २ । ३२ ॥

II.32. śauca-saṃtoṣa-tapaḥ-svādhyāya-īśvara-praṇidhānāni niyamāḥ

The niyamas (inner directives) are cleanliness, contentment, tapas, self-study and devotion to Īshvara.

सौच śauca = cleanliness, purity, purification (from √śuc, 'to purify')
संतोष saṃtoṣa = contentment (from sam+ √tuṣ, 'to become calm, satisfied')
तपस् tapas = see footnote, II.1
स्वाध्याय svādhyāya = self-study (see II.1)
ईश्वरप्रणिधान Īśvara-praṇidhāna = devotion to Īśvara (see I.23)
नियम niyama = inner directive (see II.29)

वितर्कबाधने प्रतिपक्षभावनम् ॥ २ । ३३ ॥

II.33. vitarka-bādhane pratipakṣa-bhāvanam

Removing thoughts - by the cultivation of the opposite.

वितर्क vitarka = thought, supposition, doubt, uncertainty (see I.17)
बाधन bādhana = oppressing, harassing, opposing, removing, suspending, annulment (from √bādh, 'to press, force, drive away, repel')
प्रतिपक्ष pratipakṣa = opposite, the opposite side (from prati + √pakṣa, 'wing, fin, shoulder, side, flank')
भावन bhāvana = contemplation, cultivation (see I.28)

वितर्का हिंसादयः कृतकारितानुमोदिता लोभक्रोधमोहपूर्वका मृदुमध्याधिमात्रा दुःखाज्ञानानन्तफला इति प्रतिपक्षभावनम् ॥ २ । ३४ ॥

II.34. vitarkā hiṃsā-adayaḥ kṛta-kārita-anumoditā lobha-krodha-moha-pūrvakā mṛdu-madhya-adhimātrā duḥkha-ajñāna-ananta-phalā iti pratipakṣa-bhāvanam

Thoughts of harming and so on, whether done or caused to be done or approved; whether preceded by greed, anger or delusion; whether they be mild, moderate or intense - their endless fruits are suffering and lack of knowledge (ajñāna). Therefore - cultivation of the opposite.

वितर्क vitarka = thought, supposition, doubt, uncertainty (see I.17)
हिंसा hiṃsā = harming (see II.30)
आदि ādi = et cetera, and so on
कृत kṛta = done, made, accomplished, fulfilled (see II.22)
कारित kārita = caused to be made or done (from √kṛ, 'to do')
अनुमोदित anumodita = approved, agreeable, acceptable (from anu + √mud, 'to rejoice')
लोभ lobha = greed (from √lubh, 'to be perplexed; to desire greatly')
क्रोध krodha = anger, wrath (from √krudh, 'to make angry, provoke, irritate')
मोह moha = delusion (from √muh, 'to become stupefied, bewildered, to go astray')
पूर्वक pūrvaka = preceding (see I.20)
मृदु mṛdu = mild, gentle (see I.22)
मध्य madhya = medium (see I.22)
अधिमात्र adhimātra = intense, extreme, above measure (see I.22)
दुःख duḥkha = pain, uneasiness, suffering, sorrow (see I.31)
अज्ञान ajñāna = lack of knowledge, 'non-knowledge', ignorance (see I.8)
अनन्त ananta = endless, boundless, eternal, infinite (see II.47)
फल phala = fruit (see II.14)
इति iti = here: therefore, thus
प्रतिपक्ष pratipakṣa = opposite, the opposite side (see II.33)
भावन bhāvana = contemplation, cultivation (see I.28)

अहिंसाप्रतिष्ठायां तत्संनिधौ वैरत्यागः ॥ २ । ३५ ॥
II.35. ahiṃsā-pratiṣṭhāyāṃ tat-saṃnidhau vaira-tyāgaḥ
Near one who is grounded in non-harming, hostility is abandoned.

अहिंसा ahiṃsā = non-harming (see II.30)
प्रतिष्ठा pratiṣṭhā = grounded (see I.8)
तद् tad = that, here: one
संनिधि saṃnidhi = nearness, vicinity, presence (from sam + ni + √dhā, 'to put')
वैर vaira = enmity, hostility, animosity (from √vī, 'to fall upon, attack')
त्याग tyāga = leaving, abandoning (from √tyaj, 'to leave, abandon')

सत्यप्रतिष्ठायां क्रियाफलाश्रयत्वम् ॥ २ । ३६ ॥
II.36. satya-pratiṣṭhāyāṃ kriyā-phala-āśrayatvam
When [one is] grounded in truth, actions and their fruit are connected [to one's words].

सत्य satya = truth, truthfulness (see II.30)
प्रतिष्ठा pratiṣṭhā = grounded (see I.8)
क्रिया kriyā = action (see II.1)
फल phala = fruit (see II.14)
आश्रयत्व āśrayatva = connected, dependent (from ā + √śri, 'to lean on, rest on') āśraya: the state of which anything is closely connected or on which anything rests or depends

अस्तेयप्रतिष्ठायां सर्वरत्नोपस्थानम् ॥ २ । ३७ ॥
II.37. asteya-pratiṣṭhāyāṃ sarva-ratna-upasthānam
When grounded in 'abstaining from theft' all jewels come [to one].

अस्तेय asteya = non-stealing (see II.30)
प्रतिष्ठा pratiṣṭhā = grounded (see I.8)
सर्व sarva = all
रत्न ratna = jewel, gem, treasure (from √rā, 'to grant, bestow')
उपस्थान upasthāna = coming to, going near to (from upa + √sthā, 'to stand')

ब्रह्मचर्यप्रतिष्ठायां वीर्यलाभः ॥ २ । ३८ ॥
II.38. brahmacarya-pratiṣṭhāyāṃ vīrya-lābhaḥ
When grounded in brahmacarya (continence), vigor is attained.

ब्रह्मचर्य brahmacarya = continence (see II.30)
प्रतिष्ठा pratiṣṭhā = grounded (see I.8)
वीर्य vīrya = strength, vigor (see I.20)
लाभ lābha = obtaining, attaining (from √labh, 'to take, catch sight of, obtain')

अपरिग्रहस्थैर्ये जन्मकथंतासंबोधः ॥ २। ३९॥
II.39. aparigraha-sthairye janma-kathaṃtā-saṃbodhaḥ
When stable in non-greed, the understanding of the 'why'ness of one's birth.

अपरिग्रह aparigraha = non-greed, not-grasping (see II.30)
स्थैर्य sthairya = stability (from √sthā, 'to stand')
जन्म janma = birth, origin, life (see II.12)
कथंता kathaṃtā = why-ness, the why, the how (from katha)
संबोध saṃbodha = knowledge, perfect knowledge or understanding (from sam + √budh, 'to be awake, to understand')

शौचात् स्वाङ्गजुगुप्सा परैरसंसर्गः ॥ २। ४०॥
II.40. śaucāt sva-aṅga-jugupsā parair-asaṃsargaḥ
As a result of cleanliness there is disgust for one's own limbs and no intercourse with others.

शौच śauca = cleanliness, purity, purification (see II.32)
स्व sva = own
अङ्ग aṅga = limb (see I.31)
जुगुप्सा jugupsā = disgust, dislike, (from √gup, 'to guard, protect')
पर para = other
असंसर्ग asaṃsarga = no-contact (from a - 'not' + √sṛj, 'to emit, pour forth')

सत्त्वशुद्धिसौमनस्यैकाग्र्येन्द्रियजयात्मदर्शनयोग्यत्वानि च ॥ २। ४१॥
II.41. sattva-śuddhi-saumanasya-eka-agrya-indriya-jaya-ātma-darśana-yogyatvāni ca
[Also] purity of sattva (lucidity), cheerfulness, one-pointedness, mastery of the senses and the ability of seeing one's self.

सत्त्व sattva = purity, lightness, serenity, lucidity; one of the three guṇas (see I.16)
शुद्धि śuddhi = purity (see II.28)

सौमनस्य saumanasya = gladness, cheerfulness (from su + √man, 'to think' + as + ya)
एकाग्रय ekāgrya = one-pointedness
एक eka - one; अग्रय agrya - pointed, closely attentive
इन्द्रिय indriya = sense, faculty of sense, sense-organ (see II.18)
जय jaya = mastery - conquering, triumph, victory (from √ji, 'to win; to conquer')
आत्मन् ātman = self, spirit (see II.5)
दर्शन darśana = vision (see I.30)
योग्यत्व yogyatva = ability [yogya: 'fit for yoga']
च ca = and

संतोषादनुत्तमः सुखलाभः ॥ २ । ४२ ॥
II.42. saṃtoṣād-anuttamaḥ sukha-lābhaḥ
Through contentment, the attainment of unsurpassed joy.

संतोष saṃtoṣa = contentment (see II.32)
अनुत्तम anuttama = unsurpassed (from an + ud + tama)
सुख sukha = joy (see I.33)
लाभ lābha = attainment (see II.38)

कायेन्द्रियसिद्धिरशुद्धिक्षयात्तपसः ॥ २ । ४३ ॥
II.43. kāya-indriya-siddhir-aśuddhi-kṣayāt-tapasaḥ
Through the dwindling of impurities by tapas, Siddhis in the body and the senses.

काय kāya = the body
इन्द्रिय indriya = sense, faculty of sense, sense-organ (see II.18)
सिद्धि siddhi = complete attainment, perfection, supernatural powers (from √sidh, 'to succeed, to become perfect')
अशुद्धि aśuddhi = impurity (see II.28)
क्षय kṣaya = destruction, dwindling, diminishing (see II.28)
तपस् tapas - heating practices (see footnote, II.1)

स्वाध्यायादिष्टदेवतासंप्रयोगः ॥ २ । ४४ ॥
II.44. svādhyāyād-iṣṭa-devatā-saṃprayogaḥ
Through self-study, connection with the chosen deity.

स्वाध्याय svādhyāya = self study (see II.1)
इष्ट iṣṭa = chosen, desired (from √iṣ, 'to desire, wish, long for')
देव deva = diety, god (from √div, 'to shine')
संप्रयोग saṃprayoga = connection, union (from sam + pra + √yuj, 'to yoke, to join together')

समाधिसिद्धिरीश्वरप्रणिधानात् ॥ २ । ४५ ॥
II.45. samādhi-siddhir-īśvara-praṇidhānāt
Through devotion to Īśvara, the siddhi of samādhi.

समाधि samādhi - (see I.20)
सिद्धि siddhi = perfection (see II.43)
ईश्वरप्रणिधान Īśvara-praṇidhāna = devotion to Īśvara (see I.23)

स्थिरसुखमासनम् ॥ २ । ४६ ॥
II.46. sthira-sukham-āsanam
The āsana (posture) is stable and pleasant.

स्थिर sthira = stable (from √sthā, 'to stand')
सुख sukha = pleasant, comfortable, joyful (see I.33)
आसन āsana = posture (see II.29)

प्रयत्नशैथिल्यानन्तसमापत्तिभ्याम् ॥ २ । ४७ ॥
II.47. prayatna-śaithilya-ananta-samāpattibhyām
By relaxation of effort and by samāpatti with the infinite.

प्रयत्न prayatna = persevering effort, exertion (from pra + √yat, 'to exert one's self, endeavor; to strive') see yatna, I.13
शैथिल्य śaithilya = relaxation (from śithila, 'loose, slack, relaxed')
अनन्त ananta = endless, boundless, eternal, infinite (see II.34)
समापत्ति samāpatti = coming together, a state of mind (see I.41)

ततो द्वन्द्वानभिघातः ॥ २ । ४८ ॥
II.48. tato dvandva-anabhighātaḥ
Then [the practitioner is] untroubled by the pairs of opposites.

ततस् tatas = in that place, there, then
द्वन्द्व dvandva = pair (from dva + dva)
अनभिघात anabhighāta = un-assailed, un-attacked, uninjured, untroubled (from an (not) + abhi + √han, 'to destroy, diminish')

तस्मिन्सति श्वासप्रश्वासयोर्गतिविच्छेदः प्राणायामः ॥ २ । ४९ ॥
II.49. tasmin-sati śvāsa-praśvāsayor-gati-vicchedaḥ prāṇāyāmaḥ
When this is so, then prāṇāyāma (breath-control) - the cutting off of the movement of inhalation and exhalation.

तस्मिन् tasmin = in this
सति sati = being, existing (see II.13)
तस्मिन्सति tasmin-sati = when this is so
श्वास śvāsa = inhalation (see I.31)
प्रश्वास praśvāsa = exhalation (see I.31)
गति gati = movement, flow, course (from √gam, 'to go')
विच्छेद viccheda = interruption, cutting off, (see II.4)
प्राणायाम prāṇāyāma = breath-control (see II.29)

बाह्याभ्यन्तरस्तम्भवृत्तिर्देशकालसंख्याभिः परिदृष्टो दीर्घसूक्ष्मः ॥ २ । ५० ॥
II.50. bāhya-abhyantara-stambha-vṛttir-deśa-kāla-saṃkhyābhiḥ paridṛṣṭo dīrgha-sūkṣmaḥ
Its vṛtti is external, internal or stopped; it is observed by [categories of] place, time and number and is prolonged and subtle.

बाह्य bāhya = external, outer, exterior (from √bah, 'to increase')
अभ्यन्तर abhyantara = internal, interior, being inside (from abhi + antara)

स्तम्भ stambha[16] = stopped, fixed; (from √stambh, 'to fix firmly, stop, arrest')
वृत्ति vṛtti = activity, movement, function, wave (see I.2)
देश deśa = place (see II.31)
काल kāla = time (see I.14)
संख्या saṃkhyā = number (from sam + √khyā, 'to be known, to be named')
परिदृष्ट paridṛṣṭa = to look at, see, behold (from pari + √dṛś, 'to see')
दीर्घ dīrgha = long (see I.14)
सूक्ष्म sūkṣma = subtle (see I.44)

बाह्याभ्यन्तरविषयाक्षेपी चतुर्थः ॥ २ । ५१ ॥
II.51. bāhya-abhyantara-viṣaya-ākṣepī caturthaḥ
The fourth goes beyond the external and internal sphere.

बाह्य bāhya = external (see II.50)
अभ्यन्तर abhyantara = internal (see II.50)
विषय viṣaya = object, sphere (see I.11)
आक्षेपिन् ākṣepin = to go beyond, to be transported (from ā + √kṣip, 'to throw, to cast')
चतुर्थ caturtha = fourth (from catur, 'four')

ततः क्षीयते प्रकाशावरणम् ॥ २ । ५२ ॥
II.52. tataḥ kṣīyate prakāśa-āvaraṇam
Then the covering of the bright light fades away.

ततस् tatas = then
क्षीयते kṣīyate = to weaken, fade, wane (from √kṣi, 'to be diminished, decreased')
प्रकाश prakāśa = bright light (see II.18)
आवरण āvaraṇa = covering, veil; hiding, concealing (from ā + √vṛ, 'to cover, screen, veil, conceal, hide)

16 ***Stambha*** - a post, pillar, column; support, strengthening; fixedness, rigidity; stoppage, obstruction, suppression. Also the magical arresting of any feeling or force of hunger, thirst, or of the forces of water, fire, etc. as taught in the Tantras.

धारणासु च योग्यता मनसः ॥ २ । ५३ ॥
II.53. dhāraṇāsu ca yogyatā manasaḥ
And the mind is fit for concentration.

धारणा dhāraṇā = concentration (see II.29)
च ca = and
योग्यता yogyatā = fit, capable, suitable
मनस् manas = mind (see I.35)

स्वविषयासंप्रयोगे चित्तस्य स्वरूपानुकार इवेन्द्रियाणां प्रत्याहारः ॥ २ । ५४ ॥
II.54. sva-viṣaya-asaṃprayoge cittasya sva-rūpa-anukāra iva-indriyāṇāṃ pratyāhāraḥ
Pratyāhāra (sense withdrawal) is as if the senses are imitating the true form of the consciousness, by disuniting from their objects.

स्व sva = own
विषय viṣaya = object (see I.11)
असंप्रयोग asaṃprayoga = disuniting, disconnecting (from a - 'not' + saṃprayoga, 'connection, union') [see II.44]
चित्त citta = consciousness (see I.2)
स्वरूप sva-rūpa = own form; here: true form (see I.3)
अनुकार anukāra = imitation, resemblance (from anu + √kṛ, 'to do')
इव iva = as if, as it were
इन्द्रिय indriya = sense, faculty of sense, sense-organ (see II.18)
प्रत्याहार pratyāhāra = sense-withdrawal (see II.29)

ततः परमा वश्यतेन्द्रियाणाम् ॥ २ । ५५ ॥
II.55. tataḥ paramā vaśyatā-indriyāṇām
Then the highest control of the senses.

ततस् tatas = in that place, there, then
परमा paramā = highest, supreme (see I.40)
वश्यता vaśyatā = control, subjugation (from √vaś, 'to command' + ya + tā)
इन्द्रिय indriya = sense, faculty of sense, sense-organ (see II.18)

विभूतिपादः Chapter III - Vibhūti Pādaḥ

विभूति vibhūti = penetrating, pervading, abundant, plentiful; mighty, powerful; manifestation of might, great power, superhuman power[17]
पाद pāda = chapter

देशबन्धश्चित्तस्य धारणा ॥ ३ । १ ॥
III.1. deśa-bandhaś-cittasya dhāraṇā
Dhāraṇā (concentration) is binding consciousness to a place.

दश deśa = place (see II.31)
बन्ध bandha = binding, tying, a bond (from √bandh, 'to bind')
चित्त citta = consciousness (see I.2)
धारणा dhāraṇā = concentration (see II.29)

तत्र प्रत्ययैकतानता ध्यानम् ॥ ३ । २ ॥
III.2. tatra pratyaya-ekatānatā dhyānam
Dhyāna (meditation) is one pointed fixing of a notion there [at that place].

तत्र tatra = there (at that place)
प्रत्यय pratyaya = notion (see I.10)
एकतान eka-tāna = directed to one object only, having the mind fixed on one object only (from eka, 'one' + √tan, 'to stretch, to extend')
ध्यान dhyāna = meditation, reflection (see I.39)

17 Superhuman powers consisting of eight faculties, especially attributed to Śiva, but supposed also to be attainable by human beings: aṇiman, the power of becoming as minute as an atom; laghiman, extreme lightness; prāpti, attaining or reaching anything; prākāmya, irresistible will; mahiman, illimitable bulk; īśitā, supreme dominion; vaśitā, subjugating by magic; and kāmāvasāyitā, the suppressing of all desires.

तदेवार्थमात्रनिर्भासं स्वरूपशून्यमिव समाधिः ॥ ३ । ३ ॥
III.3. tad-eva-artha-mātra-nirbhāsaṃ sva-rūpa-śūnyam-iva samādhiḥ
Samādhi is when that shines forth as the object only, as if empty of its own form.

तद् tad = that
एव eva = verily
अर्थ artha = object (see I.28)
मात्र mātra = only, merely, just
निर्भास nirbhāsa = shining forth, illuminating (see I.43)
स्वरूप sva-rūpa = own form, true form (see I.3)
शून्य śūnya = empty, void (see I.9)
इव iva = like, as if, as it were
समाधि samādhi = the eighth limb of aṣṭaṅga yoga. (see I.20)

त्रयमेकत्र संयमः ॥ ३ । ४ ॥
III.4. trayam-ekatra saṃyamaḥ
The three together - saṃyama.[18]

त्रय traya = three (from tri, 'three')
एकत्र ekatra = in one, together (from eka, 'one')
संयम saṃyama = holding together, restraint, control (from sam + √yam, 'to hold or keep in, to restrain')

तज्जयात् प्रज्ञालोकः ॥ ३ । ५ ॥
III.5. taj-jayāt prajñā-ālokaḥ
By mastery of that, the light of prajñā.

तद् tad = that
जय jaya = mastery - conquering, triumph, victory (see II.41)
प्रज्ञा prajñā = true or transcendental wisdom (see I.20)
आलोक āloka = looking; vision; light, (from ā + √lok, 'to look')

18 The term saṃyama, which will appear twelve times in this chapter refers to an intensification and integration of the three elements: dhāraṇā (concentration), dhyāna (meditation) and samādhi.

तस्य भूमिषु विनियोगः ॥ ३ । ६ ॥

III.6. tasya bhūmiṣu viniyogaḥ

Its application is by stages.

तस्य tasya = its (see I.27)
भूमि bhūmi = step, degree, stage (from √bhū, 'to be')
विनियोग viniyoga = application (from vi + ni + √yuj, 'to yoke')

त्रयमन्तरङ्गं पूर्वेभ्यः ॥ ३ । ७ ॥

III.7. trayam-antar-aṅgaṃ pūrvebhyaḥ

These three limbs are inner, [in relation to] the previous.

त्रय traya = three (see III.4)
अन्तर् antar = within, between, amongst (as adjective, 'inner, internal')
अङ्ग aṅga = limb (see I.31)
अन्तरङ्ग antar-aṅga = interior or inner limb
पूर्व pūrva = former, earlier, previous

तदपि बहिरङ्गं निर्बीजस्य ॥ ३ । ८ ॥

III.8. tad-api bahir-aṅgaṃ nirbījasya

Even so, they are external limbs [in relation to] the seedless [samādhi].

तद् tad = that, here: they
अपि api = even so
बहिरङ्ग bahir-aṅga = external limb; relating to the exterior, external, unessential (from bahis, 'out, forth, outwards' + aṅga, 'limb')
निर्बीज nirbīja = without seed (from nir + bīja, 'seed')

व्युत्थाननिरोधसंस्कारयोरभिभवप्रादुर्भावौ निरोधक्षणचित्तान्वयो निरोधपरिणामः ॥ ३ । ९ ॥
III.9. vyutthāna-nirodha-saṃskārayor-abhibhava-prādur-bhāvau nirodha-kṣaṇa-citta-anvayo nirodha-pariṇāmaḥ
The saṃskāras of outwardness are overpowered and the saṃskāras of restraint appear. Then a moment of restraint of the consciousness. This is followed by nirodha pariṇāma[19] (Restraint Transformation).

व्युत्थान vyutthāna = outwardness, rising up, awakening, activity (from vi + ud + √sthā, 'to stand')
निरोध nirodha = restraint (see I.2)
संस्कार saṃskāra = [mental] imprint (see footnote, I.18)
भाव bhāva = becoming, being, existing (from √bhū, 'to be')
अभिभव abhibhava = disappearing; powerful; defeat, subjugation
प्रादुर् prādur = to view or light, in sight (from pra + dur, 'out of doors')
प्रादुर्भाव prādur-bhāva = come out doors, appear, become manifest
क्षण kṣaṇa = an instant, a moment (from √kṣan, 'to break')
चित्त citta = consciousness (see I.2)
अन्वय anvaya = following, succession (from anu + √i, 'to go')
परिणाम pariṇāma = change, transformation (see II.15)

19 This is a difficult sūtra, which needs elaboration. The word 'nirodha' appears three times: the first time connected to saṃskāra 'imprint', the second time to kṣan 'a moment', and the third time to pariṇāma, 'transformation'. There is some sort of process called nirodha, restraint or inwardness/inward-stillness. In this process there is first an imprint of nirodha. As we practice further the brain is capable of sustaining this imprint in time - it becomes a moment. And when even this is moment is expanded and repeated again and again a change occurs in the organic structure of the brain and in our mentality - this is pariṇāma-nirodha, where stillness is integrated into our structure, becomes part of what we are.

तस्य प्रशान्तवाहिता संस्कारात् ॥ ३ । १० ॥

III.10. tasya praśānta-vāhitā saṃskārāt

Through these saṃskāras the peaceful flow of that [consciousness].

तस्य tasya = its, his - here: through these

प्रशान्त praśānta = peaceful, calm, quiet (from pra + √śam, 'to be calm')

वाहिता vāhitā = flow (from vah, 'to bear along')

संस्कार saṃskāra = [mental] imprint (see footnote, I.18)

सर्वार्थ तैकाग्रतयोः क्षयोदयौ चित्तस्य समाधिपरिणामः ॥ ३ । ११ ॥

III.11. sarva-arthatā-ekāgratayoḥ kṣaya-udayau cittasya samādhi-pariṇāmaḥ

When there is weakening of [attention to] all objects and the rise of one-pointedness, then samādhi pariṇāma, the samādhi transformation of consciousness.

सर्व sarva = all

अर्थता arthatā = lit. 'object-ness', (see I.28)

एकाग्रता ekāgratā = one-pointedness (see II.41, ekā-agrya)

क्षय kṣaya = reduction, diminishment, fading, waning, weakening (see II.28)

उदय udaya = rising up (from ud + √i, 'to go')

चित्त citta = consciousness (see I.2)

समाधि samādhi = (see I.20)

परिणाम pariṇāma = change, transformation (see II.15)

ततः पुनः शान्तोदितौ तुल्यप्रत्ययौ चित्तस्यैकाग्रतापरिणामः ॥ ३ । १२ ॥
III.12. tataḥ punaḥ śānta-uditau tulya-pratyayau cittasya-ekāgratā-pariṇāmaḥ
Then again, when the calming down and rising notions become alike, then ekāgratā pariṇāma - the one-pointedness transformation of consciousness.

ततस् tatas = thus, hence, here: then
पुनर् punar = again
शन्त śanta = peaceful, quiet - here: 'calming down' (as the opposite of udita)
उदित udita = risen, ascended (from ud + √i, 'to go')
तुल्य tulya = equal to, similar, like (from √tul,'to weigh, to compare')
प्रत्यय pratyaya = notion (see I.10)
चित्त citta = consciousness (see I.2)
एकाग्रता ekāgratā = one-pointedness (see III.11)
परिणाम pariṇāma = change, transformation (see II.15)

एतेन भूतेन्द्रियेषु धर्मलक्षणावस्थापरिणामा व्याख्याताः ॥ ३ । १३ ॥
III.13. etena bhūta-indriyeṣu dharma-lakṣaṇa-avasthā-pariṇāmā vyākhyātāḥ
By this the transformations of dharma (characteristic), lakṣaṇa (time aspect) and avasthā (state) in the senses and elements are explained.

एतेन etena = by this
भूत bhūta = element (see II.18)
इन्द्रिय indriya = sense (see II.18)
धर्म dharma = natural law, intrinsic nature or characteristic, prescribed conduct (from dhṛ, 'to hold, maintain, preserve')
लक्षण lakṣaṇa = temporal quality, time aspect, sign, attribute (from √lakṣ, 'to characterize, define')
अवस्थ avastha = state, condition, situation (from ava + √sthā, 'to stand')

परिणाम pariṇāma = change, transformation (see II.15)
व्याख्यात vyākhyāta = explained (see I.44)

शान्तोदिताव्यपदेश्यधर्मानुपाती धर्मी ॥ ३ । १४ ॥
III.14. śānta-udita-avyapadeśya-dharma-anupātī dharmī
The dharmin (substance) follows the calming down, the rising, and undetermined dharma.

शान्त śānta = receding, calming down (see III.12)
उदित udita = rising (see III.12)
अव्यपदेश्य avyapadeśya = indeterminable, undetermined (from a +vi +apa + √diś, 'to point out')
धर्म dharma - (see III.13)
अनुपातिन् anupātin = follow, go after (see I.9)
धर्मिन् dharmin = endowed with dharma, having a characteristic nature; following the laws of dharma; a substance

क्रमान्यत्वं परिणामान्यत्वे हेतुः ॥ ३ । १५ ॥
III.15. krama-anyatvaṃ pariṇāma-anyatve hetuḥ
The reason for the difference of the transformation is the difference of sequence.

क्रम krama = a step, order, series, sequence (from √kram, 'to step')
अन्यत्व anyatva = other-ness, difference (from anya, 'other' + tva)
परिणाम pariṇāma = change, transformation (see II.15)
हेतु hetu = reason (see II.17)

परिणामत्रयसंयमादतीतानागतज्ञानम् ॥ ३ । १६ ॥
III.16. pariṇāma-traya-saṃyamād-atīta-anāgata-jñānam
By saṃyama on the three transformations - the knowledge of past and future.

परिणाम pariṇāma = change, transformation (see II.15)
त्रय traya = three (see III.4)
संयम saṃyama - (see III.4)

अतीत atīta = past (from √i, 'to go')
अनागत anāgata = not come, not arrived; the future (see II.16)
ज्ञान jñāna = knowledge (see I.8)

शब्दार्थप्रत्ययानामितरेतराध्यासात्संकरस्तत्प्रविभागसंयमात्सर्वभूतरुतज्ञानम् ॥ ३ । १७ ॥
III.17. śabda-artha-pratyayānām-itara-itara-adhyāsāt-saṃkaras-tat-pravibhāga-saṃyamāt-sarva-bhūta-ruta-jñānam
[There is a natural] mixing up of word, [intended] object and notion, as they are imposed one upon the other. By saṃyama on them seperately - knowledge of the languages of all beings.

शब्द śabda = sound, word
अर्थ artha = objective, purpose, aim, here: intended object (see I.28)
प्रत्यय pratyaya = notion (see I.10)
इतर itara = other
इतरेतर itara-itara = one on another
अध्यास adhyāsa = preside over (from adhi + √as, 'to throw, to cast')
संकर saṃkara = mixing together, confusion (from sam + √kṛ, 'to do')
तद् tad = this, that
प्रविभाग pravibhāga = separation, division, distinction (from pra + vi + √bhaj, 'to divide')
संयम saṃyama - (see III.4)
सर्व sarva = all
भूत bhūta = element, here beings, creatures (see II.18)
रुत ruta = sounded, filled with cries [of animals] (from √ru, 'to roar, howl')
ज्ञान jñāna = knowledge (see I.8)
रुतज्ञान ruta-jñāna = understanding the cries [of beasts or birds]

संस्कारसाक्षात्करणात्पूर्वजातिज्ञानम् ॥ ३ । १८ ॥
III.18. saṃskāra-sākṣāt-karaṇāt-pūrva-jāti-jñānam
By direct perception of saṃskāras - knowledge of previous births.

संस्कार saṃskāra = [mental] imprint (see footnote, I.18)
साक्षात् sākṣāt = with the eyes, with one's own eyes; making evident

to the senses (sa-akṣa, 'with eye')
करण karaṇa = doing, making, causing (from √kṛ, 'to do')
साक्षात्करण sākṣāt-karaṇa = direct perception, intuitive perception, actual feeling
पूर्व pūrva = previous
जाति jāti = birth (see II.13)
ज्ञान jñāna = knowledge (see I.8)

प्रत्ययस्य परचित्तज्ञानम् ॥ ३। १९॥
III.19. pratyayasya para-citta-jñānam
By [direct perception] of his notion - knowledge of the consciousness of another.

प्रत्यय pratyaya = notion (see I.10)
पर para = other, distant, remote, opposite
चित्त citta = consciousness (see I.2)
ज्ञान jñāna = knowledge (see I.8)

न च तत्सालम्बनं तस्याविषयीभूतत्वात् ॥ ३। २०॥
III.20. na ca tat-sa-ālambanaṃ tasya-aviṣayī-bhūtatvāt
But it (knowledge) doesn't have that [notion] together with its support, that not being the object [of saṃyama].

न na = not
च ca = and
तद् tad = that, it
सालम्बन sa-ālambana = with support, base (see I.10)
तस्य tasya = his, its (see I.27)
अविषयिन् aviṣayin = no object (from a + viṣaya, object) (see I.11)
भूतत्व bhūtatva = the state of being an element, 'being-ness' (from √bhū, 'to be')

कायरूपसंयमात्तद्ग्राह्यशक्तिस्तम्भे चक्षुःप्रकाशासंयोगेऽन्तर्धानम् ॥ ३ । २१ ॥
III.21. kāya-rūpa-saṃyamāt-tad-grāhya-śakti-stambhe cakṣuḥ-prakāśa-asaṃyoge'ntardhānam
By saṃyama on the body's form and by stopping the power of it's being perceived, by disconnecting the light [shining from the body] to the eye - invisibility.

काय kāya = the body
रूप rūpa = form
संयम saṃyama -(see III.4)
तद् tad = that
ग्राह्य grāhya = grasped, perceived (see I.41)
शक्ति śakti = power (see II.6)
स्तम्भ stambha = stopping, suppression (see II.50)
चक्षुस् cakṣus = eye (from √cakṣ, 'to appear, become visible')
प्रकाश prakāśa = light, illumination (see II.18)
असंयोग asaṃyoga = disconnection (see saṃyoga, II.17)
अन्तर्धान antardhāna = literally to put within; vanishing, disappearance, invisibility (from antar 'interior' + √dhā, 'to put')

सोपक्रमं निरुपक्रमं च कर्म तत्संयमादपरान्तज्ञानमरिष्टेभ्यो वा ॥ ३ । २२ ॥
III.22. sa-upakramaṃ nir-upakramaṃ ca karma tat-saṃyamād-apara-anta-jñānam-ariṣṭebhyo vā
Karma is close by or far away. By saṃyama upon it, or by omens - the knowledge of [the] most extreme end (death).

उपक्रम upakrama = the act of going or coming near, approach (from sa + upa + √kram, 'to step, go towards')
सोपक्रम sa-upakrama = 'with approach', close by
निरुपक्रम nir-upakrama = 'without approach', far away
च ca = and
कर्म karma = action (see I.24)
तद् tad = it, that
संयम saṃyama - (see III.4)
अपरान्त aparānta = most extreme end, death (from a + para + anta, 'end')

ज्ञान jñāna = knowledge (see I.8)
अरिष्ट ariṣṭa = misfortune, sign or symptom of approaching death (from a + √riṣ, 'to be hurt or injured, perish, be lost')
वा vā = or

मैत्र्यादिषु बलानि ॥ ३ । २३ ॥
III.23. maitry-ādiṣu balāni
[By saṃyama] on friendliness and so on - powers.

मैत्री maitrī = friendliness (see I.33)
आदि ādi = and so on, etc.
बल bala = strength, power

बलेषु हस्तिबलादीनि ॥ ३ । २४ ॥
III.24. baleṣu hasti-bala-ādīni
[By saṃyama] on powers - power as of an elephant and so on.

बल bala = strength, power
हस्तिन् hastin = an elephant, (from hasta, 'hand, trunk [of an elephant]')
आदि ādi = and so on, etc.

प्रवृत्त्यालोकन्यासात् सूक्ष्मव्यवहितविप्रकृष्टज्ञानम् ॥ ३ । २५ ॥
III.25. pravṛtty-āloka-nyāsāt sūkṣma-vyavahita-viprakṛṣṭa-jñānam
By directing the light of [mental] activity - the knowledge of the subtle, the concealed and the distant.

प्रवृत्ति pravṛtti = activity (see I.35)
आलोक āloka = looking; vision; light, splendor (see III.5)
न्यास nyāsa = directing, fixing, applying (from ni + √as, 'to throw or cast')
सूक्ष्म sūkṣma = subtle, minute, small (see I.44)
व्यवहित vyavahita = placed apart, separated, interrupted, screened from view, concealed, covered (from vy + ava + √dhā, 'to put')
विप्रकृष्ट viprakṛṣṭa = distant, remote (from vi + pra + √kṛṣ, 'to drag away')
ज्ञान jñāna = knowledge (see I.8)

भुवनज्ञानं सूर्ये संयमात् ॥ ३ । २६ ॥
III.26. bhuvana-jñānaṃ sūrye saṃyamāt
By saṃyama on the sun - knowledge of the universe.

भुवन bhuvana = everything that exists; the world, earth, universe; place of being, abode (from √bhū, 'to be')
ज्ञान jñāna = knowledge (see I.8)
सूर्य sūrya = the sun (from svar, 'sun, sunshine, bright sky, heaven')
संयम saṃyama (see III.4)

चन्द्रे ताराव्यूहज्ञानम् ॥ ३ । २७ ॥
III.27. candre tārā-vyūha-jñānam
[By saṃyama] on the moon - knowledge of the arrangements of the stars.

चन्द्र candra = the moon (from √cand, 'to shine')
तारा tārā = star (from √tṛ, 'to cross over')
व्यूह vyūha = distribution, placing, arrangement (from √vyūh, 'to arrange')
ज्ञान jñāna = knowledge (see I.8)

ध्रुवे तद्गतिज्ञानम् ॥ ३ । २८ ॥
III.28. dhruve tad-gati-jñānam
[By saṃyama] on the pole star - knowledge of their course.

ध्रुव dhruva = fixed, immovable, the pole star (from √dhṛ, 'to hold')
तद् tad = that; here: their
गति gati = movement, flow, course (see II.49)
ज्ञान jñāna = knowledge (see I.8)

नाभिचक्रे कायव्यूहज्ञानम् ॥ ३ । २९ ॥
III.29. nābhi-cakre kāya-vyūha-jñānam
[By saṃyama] on the navel-wheel - knowledge of the structure of the body.

नाभि nābhi = the navel (from √nābh, 'an opening')
चक्र cakra = wheel (from √car, 'to move')
काय kāya = the body
व्यूह vyūha = arrangement, structure, distribution, order (see III.27)
ज्ञान jñāna = knowledge (see I.8)

कण्ठकूपे क्षुत्पिपासानिवृत्तिः ३ । ३० ॥
III.30. kaṇṭha-kūpe kṣut-pipāsā-nivṛttiḥ
[By saṃyama] on the hollow of the throat, the cessation of hunger and thirst.

कण्ठ kaṇṭha = throat, neck
कूप kūpa = hollow, cave, pit, well
क्षुध् kṣudh = to feel hunger
पिपासा pipāsā = to wish to drink; thirst (from √pā, 'to drink')
निवृत्ति nivṛtti = cessation (from ni + √vṛt, 'to turn')

कूर्मनाड्यां स्थैर्यम् ॥ ३ । ३१ ॥
III.31. kūrma-nāḍyāṃ sthairyam
[By saṃyama] on the turtle-nāḍi - stability

कूर्म kurma = turtle
नाडि nāḍi = river, channel
स्थैर्य sthairya = stability (see II.39)

मूर्धज्योतिषि सिद्धदर्शनम् ॥ ३ । ३२ ॥
III.32. mūrdha-jyotiṣi siddha-darśanam
[By saṃyama] on the light of the head - sight of the siddhas.

मूर्धन् mūrdhan = head, forehead (from √mūr, 'to become solid')
ज्योतिस् jyotis = light (see I.36)

मूर्धज्योतिषि mūrdha-jyotiṣi = brahma-randhra, 'Brahma's crevice', a suture or opening in the crown of the head through which the soul is said to depart on death.
सिद्ध siddha = one who has attained the highest object; perfected, endowed with supernatural faculties (from √sidh, 'to succeed, to become perfect')
दर्शन darśana = sight, vision (see I.30)

प्रातिभाद्वा सर्वम् ॥ ३। ३३॥
III.33. prātibhād-vā sarvam
Or by prātibha (intuition) - [knowledge] of all.

प्रातिभ prātibha = intuition, intuitive knowledge (from prāti + √bhā, 'to shine')
वा vā = or
सर्व sarva = all

हृदये चित्तसंवित् ॥ ३। ३४॥
III.34. hṛdaye citta-saṃvit
[By saṃyama] on the heart - the understanding of consciousness.

हृदय hṛdaya = heart
चित्त citta = consciousness (see I.2)
संविद् saṃvid = knowing, understanding, perception (from sam + √vid, 'to know')

सत्त्वपुरुषयोरत्यन्तासंकीर्णयोः प्रत्ययाविशेषो भोगः परार्थत्वात् स्वार्थसंयमात् पुरुषज्ञानम् ॥ ३। ३५॥
III.35. sattva-puruṣayor-atyanta-asaṃkīrṇayoḥ pratyaya-aviśeṣo bhogaḥ para-arthatvāt sva-artha-saṃyamāt puruṣa-jñānam
Bhoga is a notion that doesn't distinguish between puruṣa and sattva, which are absolutely unmixable. By saṃyama on that which is for its own purpose, from that whose purpose is for the other - knowledge of puruṣa.

Or
Bhoga is a notion that doesn't distinguish between the absolutely unmixable puruṣa and sattva. By saṃyama on its own purpose, [which is different] from the purpose of another - knowledge of puruṣa.[20]

सत्त्व sattva = purity, here sattva is awareness (buddhi) at its purest (see I.16)
पुरुष puruṣa = person, Self
अत्यन्त atyanta = excessive, very great, very strong; endless, unbroken, perpetual; absolute, perfect; absolutely, completely (from ati + anta, 'end')
असंकीर्ण asaṃkīrṇa = unmixed, (from a + saṃkīrṇa) (see I.42)
प्रत्यय pratyaya = notion (see I.10)
अविशेष aviśeṣa = not distinct, unparticular, not distinguished (see I.22)
भोग bhoga = experience, enjoyment (see II.13)
पर para = here: another
अर्थत्व arthatva = 'purpose-ness', having purpose, objective (see I.49)
स्व sva = own, one's own
अर्थ artha = objective, purpose, aim
संयम saṃyama (see III.4)
पुरुष puruṣa = person, Self
ज्ञान jñāna = knowledge (see I.8)

ततः प्रातिभश्रावणवेदनादर्शास्वादवार्ता जायन्ते ॥ ३ । ३६ ॥
III.36. tataḥ prātibha-śrāvaṇa-vedana-adarśa-āsvāda-vārtā jāyante
Thus arise intuition and [a heightened sense of] hearing, sensing, seeing, tasting and smelling.

ततस् tatas = in that place, there, thus
प्रातिभ prātibha = intuition (see III.33)

20 Note: The first translation implies that these two essences, puruṣa and sattva, cannot mix, like water and oil. The second translation implies that puruṣa is in itself an unmixable essence.

श्रावण śrāvaṇa = hearing (from √śru, 'to hear')
वेदना vedanā = sensing; perception, knowledge (from √vid, 'to know')
आदर्श ādarśa = seeing, perceiving with the eyes (from ā + √dṛs, 'to see')
आस्वाद āsvāda = tasting, enjoying (from ā + √svād, 'to taste well, to relish')
वार्ता vārtā = smelling (from √vṛt, 'to stir')
जायन्ते jāyante = arise (from √jan, 'to beget, to cause')

ते समाधावुपसर्गा व्युत्थाने सिद्धयः ॥ ३ । ३७ ॥
III.37. te samādhāv-upasargā vyutthāne siddhayaḥ
These are obstacles in samādhi but siddhis in an outward state.

ते te = they, these (from tad)
समाधि samādhi = (see I.20)
उपसर्ग upasarga = misfortune, obstacle (from upa + √sṛj, 'to emit, let fly')
व्युत्थान vyutthāna = outward, rising up, emergence (see III.9)
सिद्धि siddhi = perfection, supernatural powers (see II.43)

बन्धकारणशैथिल्यात्प्रचारसंवेदनाच्च चित्तस्य परशरीरावेशः ॥ ३ । ३८ ॥
III.38. bandha-kāraṇa-śaithilyāt-pracāra-saṃvedanāc-ca cittasya para-śarīra-āveśaḥ
By loosening the causes of bandha (being bound), and by perceiving-sensing the going-ons of the consciousness, [consciousness] can enter another's body.

बन्ध bandha = binding, tying, a bond (see III.1)
कारण kāraṇa = cause (from √kṛ, 'to do')
शैथिल्य śaithilya = loosening, relaxation (see II.47)
प्रचार pracāra = roaming, wandering; moving, conduct, behavior (from pra + √car, 'to move')
संवेदन saṃvedana = feeling, sensing (from sam + √vid, 'to know')
च ca = and
चित्त citta = consciousness (see I.2)

पर para = another
शरीर śarīra = body (from √sṛ, 'to support')
आवेश āveśa = entering, taking possession of (from ā + √viś, 'to enter')

उदानजयाज्जलपङ्ककण्टकादिष्वसङ्ग उत्क्रान्तिश्च ॥ ३ । ३९ ॥
III.39. udāna-jayāj-jala-paṅka-kaṇṭaka-ādiṣv-asaṅga utkrāntiś-ca
By mastery of the udāna [vayu], not clinging to water, mud, thorns etc., and ascending beyond [them].

उदान udāna = the upper breath - vayu belonging to head and neck from ud + √an, 'to breath')
जय jaya = mastery - conquering, triumph, victory (see II.41)
जल jala = water
पङ्क paṅka = mud, mire
कण्टक kaṇṭaka = thorn
आदि ādi = and so on, etc.
असङ्ग asaṅga = free from ties, independent, moving without obstacle, having no attachment or inclination for (from a + √sañj, 'to cling to')
उत्क्रान्ति utkrānti = stepping up to, ascending; going out; dying (from ud + √kram, 'to step')
च ca = and

समानजयाज्ज्वलनम् ॥ ३ । ४० ॥
III.40. samāna-jayāj-jvalanam
By mastery of the samāna [vayu] - radiance.

समान samāna = the vayu of the abdominal area (from sam + √an, 'to breath')
जय jaya = mastery - conquering, triumph, victory (see II.41)
ज्वलन jvalana = flaming, blazing; shinning, radiance (from √jval, 'to blaze')

श्रोत्राकाशयोः संबन्धसंयमाद्दिव्यं श्रोत्रम् ॥ ३ । ४१ ॥

III.41. śrotra-ākāśayoḥ saṃbandha-saṃyamād-divyaṃ śrotram

By saṃyama on the relationship between the ear and the space [within it] - the divine ear.

श्रोत्र śrotra = the organ of hearing, ear (from √śru, 'to hear')
आकाश ākāśa = space (from a + √kāś, 'to be visible')
संबन्ध saṃbandha = relationship, close connection or union (from sam + √bandh, 'to bind')
संयम saṃyama (see III.4)
दिव्य divya = divine, heavenly, celestial (from √div, 'to shine, be bright')

कायाकाशयोः संबन्धसंयमाल्लघुतूलसमापत्तेश्चाकाशगमनम् ॥ ३ । ४२ ॥

III.42. kāya-ākāśayoḥ saṃbandha-saṃyamāl-laghu-tūla-samāpatteś-ca-ākāśa-gamanam

By saṃyama on the relationship between the body and the space [surrounding it] and by samāpatti with [objects] light as cotton - walking in space.

काय kāya = the body
आकाश ākāśa = space (see III.41)
संबन्ध saṃbandha = relationship, close connection or union (see III.41)
संयम saṃyama - (see III.4)
लघु laghu = light, not heavy
तूल tūla = cotton
समापत्ति samāpatti = literally 'coming together', another name for samādhi (see notes, I.41)
च ca = and
गमन gamana = walking, going, moving (from √gam, 'to go, move, walk')

बहिरकल्पिता वृत्तिर्महाविदेह ततः प्रकाशावरणक्षयः ॥ ३ । ४३ ॥
III.43. bahir-akalpitā vṛttir-mahā-videha tataḥ prakāśa-āvaraṇa-kṣayaḥ
The great 'bodiless' is an unimagined and outer vṛtti. By it, the covering of the bright light fades away.

बहिस् bahis = out, forth, outwards (see III.8)
अकल्पित akalpita = not artificial, not pretended; natural, genuine, unimagined (from a + √kḷp, 'to be ordered, to be well ordered')
वृत्ति vṛtti = activity, movement, function, wave (see I.2)
महन्त् mahant = great
विदेह videha = bodiless (see I.19)
ततस् tatas = then, thus; here: by it
प्रकाश prakāśa = brightness, bright light (see II.18)
आवरण āvaraṇa = covering, veil; hiding, concealing (see II.52)
क्षय kṣaya = destruction, reduction, fading (see II.28)

स्थूलस्वरूपसूक्ष्मान्वयार्थवत्त्वसंयमाद्भूतजयः ॥ ३ । ४४ ॥
III.44. sthūla-sva-rūpa-sūkṣma-anvaya-arthavattva-saṃyamād-bhūta-jayaḥ
By saṃyama on the gross, the true form, the subtle, the connectedness and the purposefulness - mastery over the elements.

स्थूल sthūla = coarse, gross
स्वरूप sva-rūpa = own form, true form (see I.3)
सूक्ष्म sūkṣma = subtle, minute, small (see I.44)
अन्वय anvaya = following, succession, connection, association, being linked to, natural order (see III.9)
अर्थवत्त्व arthavattva = having purpose, significance, importance, purposefulness (from artha + vat + tva)
संयम saṃyama - (see III.4)
भूत bhūta = element (see II.18)
जय jaya = mastery - conquering, triumph, victory (see II.41)

ततोऽणिमादिप्रादुर्भावः कायसंपत्तद्धर्मानभिघातश्च ॥ ३ । ४५ ॥

III.45. tato'ṇima-ādi-prādur-bhāvaḥ kāya-saṃpat-tad-dharma-anabhighātaś-ca

Then [siddhis] such as atomization[21], etc., come about, and there is perfection of the body and the unassailabilty of its (dharmas) characteristics.

ततस् tatas = then, thus
अणिमन् aṇiman = atomization (see footnote)
आदि ādi = and so on, etc.
प्रादुर्भाव prādur-bhāva = come about, become manifest (see III.9)
काय kāya = the body
संपद् saṃpad = completion, perfection (from sam + √pad, 'to fall')
तद् tad = that, there
धर्म dharma =(see III.13) here: characteristics
अनभिघात anabhighāta = unassailed, unattacked, uninjured (see II.48)
च ca = and

रूपलावण्यबलवज्रसंहननत्वानि कायसंपत् ॥ ३ । ४६ ॥

III.46. rūpa-lāvaṇya-bala-vajra-saṃhananatvāni kāya-saṃpat

The perfection of the body - beautiful form, grace, power and the compactness of a thunderbolt.

रूप rūpa = form
लावण्य lāvaṇya = beauty, loveliness, charm (from √lū, 'to cut' + nya)
बल bala = strength, power
वज्र vajra = thunderbolt (from √vaj, 'to be hard or strong')
संहननत्व saṃhananatva = compactness, solidity, firmness (from sam + √han, 'to smite' + na + tva)
काय kāya = the body
संपद् saṃpad = success, completion, perfection (see III.45)

21 ***Aṇiman*** - minuteness, fineness, thinness; atomic nature; the power (siddhi) of becoming as small as an atom; the smallest particle.

ग्रहणस्वरूपास्मितान्वयार्थवत्त्वसंयमादिन्द्रियजयः ॥ ३ । ४७ ॥

III.47. grahaṇa-sva-rūpa-asmitā-anvaya-arthavattva-saṃyamād-indriya-jayaḥ

By saṃyama on grasping, the true form, 'I am'ness', connectedness and purposefulness - mastery over the senses.

ग्रहण grahaṇa = grasping, perception (see I.41)
स्वरूप sva-rūpa = own form, true form (see I.3)
अस्मिता asmitā = literally - 'I am'ness (see II.3)
अन्वय anvaya = connection, connectedness (see III.9)
अर्थवत्त्व arthavattva = purposefulness, having purpose, objective (see III.44)
संयम saṃyama - (see III.4)
इन्द्रिय indriya = sense, faculty of sense, sense-organ (see II.18)
जय jaya = mastery - conquering, triumph, victory (see II.41)

ततो मनोजवित्वं विकरणभावः प्रधानजयश्च ॥ ३ । ४८ ॥

III.48. tato mano-javitvaṃ vikaraṇa-bhāvaḥ pradhāna-jayaś-ca

By this speed as of the mind, a state lacking sense organs and mastery of the essential components of the universe.

ततस् tatas = then, thus, by this
मनस् manas = mind (see I.35)
जवित javitva = running (from √jū, 'to be quick' + i + tva)
विकरण vikaraṇa = lacking sense organs (from vi + √kṛ, 'to do')
भाव bhāva = state (see III.9)
प्रधान pradhāna = root of prakṛti, original source of the visible or material universe (from pra + √dhā, 'to put')
जय jaya = mastery - conquering, triumph, victory (see II.41)
च ca = and

सत्त्वपुरुषान्यताख्यातिमात्रस्य सर्वभावाधिष्ठातृत्वं सर्वज्ञातृत्वं च ॥ ३ । ४९ ॥

III.49. sattva-puruṣa-anyatā-khyāti-mātrasya sarva-bhāva-adhiṣṭhātṛtvaṃ sarva-jñātṛtvaṃ ca

By merely perceiving the otherness of sattva and puruṣa, supremacy over all states of existence and all knowledge.

सत्त्व sattva = purity, here sattva is awareness (buddhi) at its purest (see I.16)
पुरुष puruṣa = person, Self
अन्यता anyatā = otherness, difference (from √anya, 'other' + tā)
ख्याति khyāti = to perceive, to have vision (see I.16)
मात्र mātra = merely, just, only
सर्व sarva = all
भाव bhāva = state (see III.9)
अधिष्ठातृत्व adhiṣṭhātṛtva = supremacy (from adhi + √sthā, 'to stand' + tṛ + tva)
ज्ञातृत्व jñātṛtva = 'knowing-ness', possessing all knowledge, omniscience (from jñātṛ, 'one who knows' + tva)
च ca = and

तद्वैराग्यादपि दोषबीजक्षये कैवल्यम् ॥ ३ । ५० ॥

III.50. tad-vairāgyād-api doṣa-bīja-kṣaye kaivalyam

By non-attachment even to that, the seeds of defects diminishing, then kaivalya - aloneness.

तद् tad = that
वैराग्य vairāgya = non-attachment (see I.12)
अपि api = also, even so
दोष doṣa = fault, vice, deficiency, defect (from √duṣ, 'to become bad or corrupted')
बीज bīja = seed
क्षय kṣaya = destruction, reduction, waning (see II.28)
कैवल्य kaivalya = aloneness (see footnote, II.25)

स्थान्युपनिमन्त्रणे सङ्गस्मयाकरणं पुनरनिष्टप्रसङ्गात् ॥ ३ । ५१ ॥
III.51. sthāny-upanimantraṇe saṅga-smaya-akaraṇaṃ punar-aniṣṭa-prasaṅgāt
Even then with the invitation of high placed [beings], there is no cause for attachment or pride because of the undesired and repeated inclination [of falling].

स्थानिन् sthānin = having a place, occupying a [high] place (from √sthā, 'to stand')
उपनिमन्त्रण upanimantraṇa = invitation (from upa + ni + √man, 'to think' + tra + na)
सङ्ग saṅga = sticking, clinging to; attachment (see asaṅga, III.39)
स्मय smaya = arrogance, conceit, pride (from √smi, 'to be proud or arrogant')
अकरण akaraṇa = absence of action, here: no cause (from a + √kṛ, 'to do')
पुनर् punar = again and again, repeatedly
अनिष्ट aniṣṭa = undesirable, disadvantageous (from an + √iṣ, 'to desire')
प्रसङ्ग prasaṅga = inclination, fondness for (from pra + sañj, 'to cling to')

क्षणतत्क्रमयोः संयमाद्विवेकजं ज्ञानम् ॥ ३ । ५२ ॥
III.52. kṣaṇa-tat-kramayoḥ saṃyamād-viveka-jaṃ jñānam
By saṃyama on the moment and the sequence - the knowledge born of discernment.

क्षण kṣaṇa = an instant, a moment (see III.9)
तद् tad = here: the
क्रम krama = a step, order, series, sequence (see III.15)
संयम saṃyama - (see III.4)
विवेक viveka = discernment (see II.26)
ज ja = born (see I.50)
ज्ञान jñāna = knowledge (see I.8)

जातिलक्षणदेशैरन्यतानवच्छेदात्तुल्ययोस्ततः प्रतिपत्तिः ॥ ३ । ५३ ॥

III.53. jāti-lakṣaṇa-deśair-anyatā-anavacchedāt-tulyayos-tataḥ pratipattiḥ

Then the ability to differentiate between those that seem the same because they cannot be distinguished by birth, temporal quality or point in space.

जाति jāti = birth, class, species (see II.13)
लक्षण lakṣaṇa = temporal quality (see III.13)
देश deśa = point in space, place, location (see II.31)
अन्यता anyatā = difference (see III.49)
अनवच्छेद् anavaccheda = unbound, un-separated, indistinct (see I.26)
तुल्य tulya = equal to, similar, like (see III.12)
ततस् tatas = thus, hence, here: then
प्रतिपत्ति pratipatti = perception, observation, knowledge (from prati + √pad, 'to fall')

तारकं सर्वविषयं सर्वथाविषयमक्रमं चेति विवेकजं ज्ञानम् ॥ ३ । ५४ ॥

III.54. tārakaṃ sarva-viṣayaṃ sarvathā-viṣayam-akramaṃ ca-iti viveka-jaṃ jñānam

The knowledge born of discernment is the deliverer - all objects and all time are its objective and it is without sequence.

तारक tāraka = enabling to cross over, rescuing, liberating, saving, delivering (from √tṛ, 'to cross over')
सर्व sarva = all
विषय viṣaya = object, sphere (see I.11)
सर्वथा sarvathā = all of time (past, present and future), wholeness, totality, completeness, everything
अक्रम akrama = without order, without sequence, confusion; not happening successively, happening at once (see III.15)
च ca = and
इति iti = here iti serves as the dash
विवेक viveka = discernment (see II.15)
ज ja = born (see I.50)
ज्ञान jñāna = knowledge (see I.8)

सत्त्वपुरुषयोः शुद्धिसाम्ये कैवल्यमिति ॥ ३ । ५५ ॥
III.55. sattva-puruṣayoḥ śuddhi-sāmye kaivalyam-iti
When the sattva and the puruṣa are of the same purity - kaivalya, aloneness.

सत्त्व sattva = purity, here sattva is awareness (buddhi) at its purest (see I.16)
पुरुष puruṣa = person, Self
शुद्धि śuddhi = purity (from √śudh, 'to be cleansed, purified')
साम्य sāmya = sameness, equality, evenness (from √sama, 'same')
कैवल्य kaivalya = aloneness (see footnote, II.25)
इति iti = here iti serves as the dash

कैवल्य पाद् Chapter IV - Kaivalya Pāda

कैवल्य kaivalya = aloneness (see footnote, II.25)
पाद् pāda = chapter

जन्मौषधिमन्त्रतपःसमाधिजाः सिद्धयः ॥ ४ । १ ॥
IV.1. janma-oṣadhi-mantra-tapaḥ-samādhi-jāḥ siddhayaḥ
The siddhis are the result of birth, herbs, mantra, tapas and samādhi.

जन्मन् janman = birth, origin, life (see II.12)
ओषधि oṣadhi = plant, herb, medicinal herb
मन्त्र mantra = 'instrument of thought'; a mystical verse or magical formula (from √man, 'to think')
तपस् tapas - (see footnote, II.1)
समाधि samādhi = (see I.20)
ज ja = born (see I.50)
सिद्धि siddhi = complete attainment, perfection, supernatural powers (see II.43)

जात्यन्तरपरिणामः प्रकृत्यापूरात् ॥ ४ । २ ॥
IV.2. jāty-antara-pariṇāmaḥ prakṛty-āpūrāt
The transformation into another type of existence [is possible] because of nature's abundance.

जाति jāti = birth (see II.13)
अन्तर antara = other, different from, (from anta, 'end, limit, boundary')
परिणाम pariṇāma = change, transformation (see II.15)
प्रकृति prakṛti = nature (see I.19)
आपूर āpūra = abundance, filling-in, excess (from ā + √pṛ, 'to surpass, excel')

निमित्तमप्रयोजकं प्रकृतीनां वरणभेदस्तु ततः क्षेत्रिकवत् ॥ ४ । ३ ॥
IV.3. nimittam-aprayojakaṃ prakṛtīnāṃ varaṇa-bhedas-tu tataḥ kṣetrikavat
The instrumental cause does not impel nature's [evolving], it only makes a breach in the barrier as the farmer does [for irrigating his field].

निमित्त nimitta = instrumental cause, (from ni + √mā, 'to measure, estimate')
अप्रयोजक aprayojaka = not causing or effecting, aimless, not impel (from a + pra + √yuj, 'to yoke, joint together')
प्रकृति prakṛti = nature (see I.19)
वरण varaṇa = obstruction, barrier, mound
भेद bheda = breaking, splitting, distinction, (from √bhid, 'to split, cleave; to distinguish')
तु tu = but, rather
ततस् tatas = thus
क्षेत्रिक kṣetrika = the owner of a field, farmer (from √kṣi, 'to posses' + ka)

निर्माणचित्तान्यस्मितामात्रात् ॥ ४ । ४ ॥
IV.4. nirmāṇa-cittāny-asmitā-mātrāt
Created consciousnesses result from 'I am'ness only.

निर्माण nirmāṇa = forming, making, creating (from nir + √mā, 'to measure, estimate')
चित्त citta = consciousness (see I.2)
अस्मिता asmitā = literally - 'I am'ness (see II.3)
मात्र mātra = merely, scarcely, just, only

प्रवृत्तिभेदे प्रयोजकं चित्तमेकमनेकेषाम् ॥ ४ । ५ ॥
IV.5. pravṛtti-bhede prayojakaṃ cittam-ekam-anekeṣām
There are distinct activities, yet it is one consciousness that impels the many.

प्रवृत्ति pravṛtti = activity (see I.35)
भेद bheda = breaking, splitting, distinction, sort (see IV.3)
प्रयोजक prayojaka = causing, effecting, leading to, impelling (see IV.3)
चित्त citta = consciousness (see I.2)
एक eka = one
अनेक aneka = not one, many, much (from an + eka)

तत्र ध्यानजमनाशयम् ॥ ४ । ६ ॥
IV.6. tatra dhyāna-jam-anāśayam
That which is born of meditation leaves no deposit.

तत्र tatra = here: that
ध्याना dhyānā = meditation, thought, reflection (see I.39)
ज ja = born (see I.50)
अनाशय anāśaya = no deposit (from an, 'no, without' + āśaya, 'deposit')

कर्माशुक्लाकृष्णं योगिनस्त्रिविधमितरेषाम् ॥ ४ । ७ ॥
IV.7. karma-aśukla-akṛṣṇaṃ yoginas-trividham-itareṣām
The karma of yogis is neither white nor black. The other's [karma] is of three kinds.

कर्म karma = action, destiny (see III.22)
अशुक्ल aśukla = not white (from a + √śuc, 'to purify')
अकृष्ण akṛṣṇa = not black (from a + √kṛṣṇa, 'black, dark, dark blue')
योगिन् yogin = a yogi
त्रिविध trividha = triple, three kinds, threefold (from tri, 'three' + vidha)
इतर itara = other

ततस्तद्विपाकानुगुणानामेवाभिव्यक्तिर्वासनानाम् ॥ ४ । ८ ॥
IV.8. tatas-tad-vipāka-anuguṇānām-eva-abhivyaktir-vāsanānām
Therefore, the manifestation of only those vāsanās which correspond to the ripening of [their karma].

ततस् tatas = therefore, then
तद् tad = this
विपाक vipāka = ripens, bears fruit (see I.24)
अनुगण anuguṇa = having similar qualities, corresponding to
एव eva = only
अभिव्यक्ति abhivyakti = manifestation (from abhi + vi + √añj, 'to make clear')
वासना vāsanā = inherent character traits

जातिदेशकालव्यवहितानामप्यानन्तर्यं स्मृतिसंस्कारयोरेकरूपत्वत् ॥ ४ । ९ ॥
IV.9. jāti-deśa-kāla-vyavahitānām-apy-ānantaryaṃ smṛti-saṃskārayor-eka-rūpatvat
Because of uniformity between memory and saṃskāras there is (a) sequential relation [of karmic cause and effect] even if they are separated by birth, place and time.

जाति jāti = birth (see II.13)
देश deśa = place (see II.31)
काल kāla = time (see I.14)
व्यवहित vyavahita = separated (see III.25)
अपि api = also, even
आनन्तर्य ānantarya = immediate sequence or succession; proximity, absence of interval (from an + antar + ya)
स्मृति smṛti = memory (see I.6)
संस्कार saṃskāra = [mental] imprint (see footnote, I.18)
एकरूपत्व eka-rūpatva = uniformity (from eka, 'one' + rūpa, 'form' + tva)

तासामनादित्वं चाशिषो नित्यत्वात् ॥ ४ । १० ॥

IV.10. tāsām-anāditvaṃ ca-āśiṣo nityatvāt

And these have no beginning because desire is eternal.

तासाम् tāsām = these (from tad)

अनादित्व anāditva = the sate of having no beginning (from an+ ādi + tva)

च ca = and

आशिस् āśis = desire, asking for, prayer, wish (from ā + √śās, to direct, order, command')

नित्यत्व nityatva = perpetually, constantly, eternal (from nitya + tva)

हेतुफलाश्रयालम्बनैः संगृहीतत्वादेषामभावे तदभावः ॥ ४ । ११ ॥

IV.11. hetu-phala-āśraya-ālambanaiḥ saṃgṛhītatvād-eṣām-abhāve tad-abhāvaḥ

They are held together by cause and effect, substratum and support. If these cease to be then those cease to be.

हेतु hetu = impulse, motive, cause (see II.17)

फल phala = fruit, consequence, effect

आश्रय āśraya = substratum, support, the state of which anything is closely connected or on which anything rests or depends (see II.36)

आलम्बन ālambana = support (see I.10)

संगृहीतत्व saṃgṛhītatva = held together, grasping (from sam + √grah, to grasp)

एषाम् eṣām = these (from etad)

अभाव abhāva = non-becoming, ceasing to be (see I.10)

तद् tad = that, here - those

अतीतानागतं स्वरूपतोऽस्त्यध्वभेदाद्धर्माणाम् ॥ ४ । १२ ॥
IV.12. atīta-anāgataṃ sva-rūpato'sty-adhva-bhedād-dharmāṇām
Past and future exist in their own form because of the differences in the paths of dharmas.

अतीत atīta = gone by, past (see III.16)
अनागत anāgata = the future (see II.16)
स्वरूपतस् sva-rūpatas = own form, essence
अस्ति asti = is, exists (from √as, to be)
अध्वन् adhvan = path (from √dhāv, to flow, stream, run)
भेद bheda = split, distinct, difference (see IV.3)
धर्म dharma = here characteristics (see III.13)

ते व्यसूक्ष्मा गुणात्मानः ॥ ४ । १३ ॥
IV.13. te vyakta-sūkṣmā guṇa-ātmānaḥ
These are manifest or subtle and are of the nature of the guṇas.

ते te = these (from tad)
व्य vyakta = manifest (see IV.8)
सूक्ष्म sūkṣma = subtle, minute, small (see I.44)
गुण guṇa = the three main building blocks , sattva, rajas and tamas of prakṛti, (see footnote I.16)
आत्मन् ātman = self, spirit, nature, essence

परिणामैकत्वाद्वस्तुतत्त्वम् ॥ ४ । १४ ॥
IV.14. pariṇāma-ekatvad-vastu-tattvam
The 'that'ness of a thing is due to the singularity of its transformation.

परिणाम pariṇāma = change, transformation (see II.15)
एकत्व ekatva = singularity, unity
वस्तु vastu = object, thing (see I.9)
तत्त्व tattva = true principle, truth, reality

वस्तुसाम्ये चित्तभेदात्तयोर्विभः पन्थाः ॥ ४ । १५ ॥

IV.15. vastu-sāmye citta-bhedāt-tayor-vibhaktaḥ panthāḥ

While the thing [remains] the same, consciousnesses are different, therefore the paths of these are separate.

वस्तु vastu = object, thing (see I.9)
साम्य sāmya = sameness, equality, evenness (see III.55)
चित्त citta = consciousness (see I.2)
भेद् bheda = breaking, splitting, difference, kind, (from √bhid, 'to split, cleave, to distinguish') (see IV.3)
तयोः tayoḥ = of both (from tad)
विभ vibhakta = divided, separated , (from vi + √bhaj, to divide)
पन्थन् panthan = path (from √path to bring into)

न चैकचित्ततन्त्रं वस्तु तदप्रमाणकं तदा किं स्यात् ॥ ४ । १६ ॥

IV.16. na ca-eka-citta-tantraṃ vastu tad-apramāṇakaṃ tadā kiṃ syāt

'A thing is not dependent on one consciousness' - This is unprovable. If this was so, what would it [the thing] be?

न na = not
च ca = and
एक eka = one
चित्त citta = consciousness (see I.2)
तन्त्र tantra = a loom, essential part, depending on (from √tan, extend)
वस्तु vastu = thing, object (see I.9)
तद् tad = that, this
अप्रमाणक apramāṇaka = unprovable (from a + pra + √mā, to measure + na + ka)
तदा tadā = this , then
किम् kim = what
स्यात् syāt = would be (from √as, to be)

तदुपरागापेक्षित्वाच्चित्तस्य वस्तु ज्ञाताज्ञातम् ॥ ४ । १७ ॥
IV.17. tad-uparāga-apekṣitvāc-cittasya vastu jñāta-ajñātam
Depending on consciousness's expectation of being colored by it, a thing is known or not known.

तद् tad = that, it
उपराग uparāga = colored (from upa + √raj, color, excited)
अपेक्षित्व apekṣitva = looking for, hope, expectation (from apa + √īkṣ, to look + tva)
चित्त citta = consciousness (see I.2)
वस्तु vastu = object, thing (see I.9)
ज्ञात jñāta = known (from √jña, 'to know')
अज्ञात ajñāta = not known (from a + √jña, 'to know')

सदा ज्ञाताश्चित्तवृत्तयस्तत्प्रभोः पुरुषस्यापरिणामित्वात् ॥ ४ । १८ ॥
IV.18. sadā jñātās-citta-vṛttayas-tat-prabhoḥ puruṣasya-apariṇāmitvāt
The vṛttis of the consciousness are always known to its master, the puruṣa, which is unchanging.

सदा sadā =always
ज्ञात jñāta = known (see IV.17)
चित्त citta = consciousness (see I.2)
वृत्ति vṛtti = activity, movement, function, wave (see I.2)
तद् tad = that, it
प्रभु prabhu = master (from pra + √bhū, to be)
पुरुष puruṣa = person, Self
अपरिणामित्व apariṇāmitva = unchanging (from a + pariṇāma, see II.15)

न तत्स्वाभासं दृश्यत्वात् ॥ ४ । १९ ॥
IV.19. na tat-sva-ābhāsaṃ dṛśyatvāt
It (consciousness) does not shine of itself because it is the seen.

न na = not
तद् tad = here: it

स्व sva = own, one's own
आभास ābhāsa = shine (from a + bhās - to shine)
दृश्यत्व dṛśyatva = the seen (from √dṛś, to see) (see II.17)

एकसमये चौभयानवधारणम् ॥ ४ । २० ॥
IV.20. eka-samaye ca-ubhaya-anavadhāraṇam
And there cannot be a comprehending of both at the same time.

एक eka = one
समय samaya = same (see II.31)
eke samaya - at the same time, simoultenously
च ca = and
उभय ubhaya = both
अनवधारण anavadhārana = non comprehending, non cognizing (from an + ava + √dhṛ, to hold)

चित्तान्तरदृश्ये बुद्धिबुद्धेरतिप्रसङ्गः स्मृतिसंकरश्च ॥ ४ । २१ ॥
IV.21. citta-antara-dṛśye buddhi-buddher-atiprasaṅgaḥ smṛti-saṃkaraś-ca
If consciousness was seen by another, there would be excessive connectiveness between one awareness and another awareness and confusion of memory.

चित्त citta = consciousness (see I.2)
अन्तर antara = other, different from, (from anta, 'end, boundary') (see IV.2)
दृश्य dṛśya = the seen (see II.17)
बुद्धि buddhi = awareness (from √budh, to be aware)
अतिप्रसङ्ग atiprasaṅga = exceesive connectiveness, (from ati + pra + √sañj, to adhere)
स्मृति smṛti = memory (see I.6)
संकर saṃkara = mixing together, confusion (from sam + √kṛ, 'to do') (see III.17)
च ca = and

चितेरप्रतिसंक्रमायास्तदाकारापत्तौ स्वबुद्धिसंवेदनम् ॥ ४ । २२ ॥

IV.22. citer-apratisaṃkramāyās-tad-ākāra-āpattau sva-buddhi-saṃvedanam

There is knowledge of one's own awareness (buddhi) when the unroaming higher consciousness takes on that appearance [of consciousness].

चिति citi = higher consciousness (from cit, - to be aware)
अप्रतिसंक्रम apratisaṃkrama = unroaming (see III.15)
तद् tad = that
आकार ākāra = takes, makes (from a + √kṛ, - to do , act)
आपत्ति āpatti = appearance (from a + √pat, to appear, to fall towards)
स्व sva = own, one's own
बुद्धि buddhi = awareness, high intelligence or mind (see IV.21)
संवेदन saṃvedana = perceiving, feeling, sensing, knowing (from sam + √vid, 'to know') (see III.38)

द्रष्टृदृश्योपरं चित्तं सर्वार्थम् ॥ ४ । २३ ॥

IV.23. draṣṭṛ-dṛśya-uparaktaṃ cittaṃ sarva-artham

When the consciousness is colored by the see'er and the seen [it perceives] all objectives.

द्रष्टृ draṣṭṛ = the see'er (see I.3)
दृश्य dṛśya = the seen (see II.17)
उपर uparakta = colored (from upa + √raj, to be excited)
चित्त citta = consciousness (see I.2)
सर्व sarva = all
अर्थ artha = objective, purpose, aim

तदसंख्येयवासनाभिश्चित्रमपि परार्थं संहत्यकारित्वात् ॥ ४ । २४ ॥

IV.24. tad-asaṃkhyeya-vāsanābhiś-citram-api para-arthaṃ saṃhatya-kāritvāt

That [consciousness], though spotted by countless vasanas, exists for another purpose. It functions by combinations [with others, like senses and objects].

तद् tad =that
असंख्येय asaṃkhyeya =countless (from a + sam + √khyā, to be mentioned)
वासना vāsanā = latent impressions, inherent character traits [see footnote, Vyāsa I.24]
चित्र citra =spotted, speckled (from √cit, to be visible)
अपि api = also, though
पर para = another
अर्थ artha = objective, purpose, aim
संहत्य saṃhatya = joined. Combined: here - combinations (from sam + √han, to strike)
कारित्व kāritva = activity (from √kṛ - to do, act)

विशेषदर्शिन आत्मभावभावनाविनिवृत्तिः ॥ ४ । २५ ॥
IV.25. viśeṣa-darśina ātma-bhāva-bhāvanā-vinivṛttiḥ
For him who sees the distinction [between sattva and puruṣa] there is a ceasing of contemplation concerning his own states of being.

विशेष viśeṣa = difference, distinction (see I.22)
दर्शिन् darśin = seeing, one who sees (from drś, 'to see')
आत्मन् ātman = self
भाव bhāva =being, states of being (from √bhū, 'to be') (see III.9)
भावना bhāvanā = = contemplation, cultivation, (from √bhū, 'to be')
विनिवृत्ति vinivṛtti = ceasing (from vi + ni + √vṛt, to turn)

तदा विवेकनिम्नं कैवल्यप्राग्भारं चित्तम् ॥ ४ । २६ ॥
IV.26. tadā viveka-nimnaṃ kaivalya-prāgbhāraṃ cittam
Then consciousness is inclined towards viveka and is leaning towards aloneness.

तदा tadā = then
विवेक viveka = discernment (see II.26)
निम्न nimna = inclines, (from ni + √nam, to bend)
कैवल्य kaivalya = aloneness (see footnote, II.25)

प्राक् prāk = forwards, to the east
भार bhāra = bending, leaning, not far from yoga (from √bhṛ, to bear)
चित्त citta = consciousness (see I.2)

तच्छिद्रेषु प्रत्ययान्तराणि संस्कारेभ्यः ॥ ४ । २७ ॥
IV.27. tac-chidreṣu pratyaya-antarāṇi saṃskārebhyaḥ
In the gaps, other notions from the saṃskāras [arise].

तद् tad = that, here : the
छिद्र chidra = gap (from √chid, to cut)
प्रत्यय pratyaya = notion (see I.10)
अन्तर antara = other, (from anta, 'end, limit, boundary') (see IV.2)
संस्कार saṃskāra = [mental] imprint (see footnote, I.18)

हानमेषां क्लेशवदुक्तम् ॥ ४ । २८ ॥
IV.28. hānam-eṣāṃ kleśavad-uktam
Their relinquishing, as explained [concerning] the kleśas.

हान hāna = the act of abandoning, relinquishing, giving up (see II.25)
एषाम् eṣām = their (from etad)
क्लेशवत् kleśa-vat =like the kleshas, = cause of pain or afflictions (from √kliś, 'to torment, cause pain; to be afflicted') (see I.24, kleśa)
ukta = explained

प्रसंख्यानेऽप्यकुसीदस्य सर्वथा विवेकख्यातेर्धर्ममेघः समाधिः ॥ ४ । २९ ॥
IV.29. prasaṃkhyāne'py-akusīdasya sarvathā viveka-khyāter-dharma-meghaḥ samādhiḥ
For him who is uninterested, even in being elevated, [having] always the vision of discernment; the 'cloud of dharma' samādhi.

प्रसंख्यान prasaṃkhyāna =being elevated, elevation
अपि api = even
अकुसीद akusīda = uninterested , not wanting gain
सर्वथा sarvathā = always (see III.54)

विवेक viveka = discernment (see II.26)
ख्याति khyāti = to perceive, to have vision (see I.16)
धर्म dharma = natural law, intrinsic nature or characteristic, prescribed conduct (from dhṛ, 'to hold, maintain, preserve')
मेद्द megha = cloud (from √mih, to make water)
समाधि samādhi =(from sam + ā + √dhā, 'to put') (see I.20)

ततः क्लेशकर्मनिवृत्तिः ॥ ४ । ३० ॥
IV.30. tataḥ kleśa-karma-nivṛttiḥ
Then the ceasing of the kleśas and the karma.

ततस् tatas = then
क्लेश kleśa = cause of pain or afflictions (see I.24)
कर्म karma = (see III.22)
निवृत्ति nivṛtti =ceasing (see II.30)

तदा सर्वावरणमलापेतस्य ज्ञानस्यानन्त्याज्ज्ञेयमल्पम् ॥ ४ । ३१ ॥
IV.31. tadā sarva-āvaraṇa-mala-apetasya jñānasya-ānantyāj-jñeyam-alpam
Then, when all the covers of impurity have been removed - endlessness of knowledge- There is little [left] to be known.

तदा tadā = then
सर्व sarva = all
आवरण āvaraṇa = covering, veil; hiding, concealing (see II.52)
मल mala = dirt, filth, dust, impurity
अपेत apeta = removed (from apa + √i, to go)
ज्ञान jñāna = knowledge (see I.8)
आनन्त्य ānantya = endlessness, infinity (from an + anta -end+ ya)
ज्ञेय jñeya = to be know (from √jña, to know)
अल्प alpa = little

ततः कृतार्थानां परिणामक्रमसमाप्तिर्गुणानाम् ॥ ४ । ३२ ॥
IV.32. tataḥ kṛta-arthānāṃ pariṇāma-krama-samāptir-guṇānām
Then as the guṇas having fulfilled their purpose, the sequences of their transformation [come to] an end.

ततस् tatas =thence, then
कृत kṛta = done, made, accomplished, fulfilled (see II.22)
अर्थ artha = objective, purpose, aim
परिणाम pariṇāma = change, transformation (see II.15)
क्रम krama = a step, sequence (from √kram, 'to step') (see III.15)
समाप्ति samāpti = end, accomplishment, completion,
गुण guṇa (see footnote I.16)

क्षणप्रतियोगी परिणामापरान्तनिर्ग्राह्यः क्रमः ॥ ४ । ३३ ॥
IV.33. kṣaṇa-pratiyogī pariṇāma-apara-anta-nirgrāhyaḥ kramaḥ
The sequence is correlated to the moment and is grasped as such at the final end of transformation.

क्षण kṣaṇa = moment (see III.9)
प्रतियोगिन् pratiyogin = correlated (from prati + √yuj, to join, connect)
परिणाम pariṇāma = change, transformation (see II.15)
अपरन्त aparanta = final end, death (see III.22)
निर्ग्राह्य nirgrāhya = grasped (from nir + √grah, to grasp)
क्रम krama = a step, series, sequence (from √kram, 'to step')
(see III.15)

पुरुषार्थशून्यानां गुणानां प्रतिप्रसवः कैवल्यं स्वरूपप्रतिष्ठा वा चितिशक्तिरिति ॥ ४ । ३४ ॥
IV.34. puruṣa-artha-śūnyānāṃ guṇānāṃ pratiprasavaḥ kaivalyaṃ sva-rūpa-pratiṣṭhā vā citi-śaktir-iti
Kaivalya (aloneness) is the involution of the guṇas [because they are] devoid of purpose for the puruṣa, or it is the grounding of the power of higher consciousness in its own form. Finis.

पुरुष puruṣa = person, self
अर्थ artha = objective, purpose, aim (see I.28)

शून्य śūnya = empty, devoid (see I.9)
गुण guṇa = see footnote I.16
प्रतिप्रसव pratiprasava = re-emergence, involution (see II.10)
कैवल्य kaivalya = aloneness (see footnote, II.25)
स्वरूप sva-rūpa = own form, true from (see I.3)
प्रतिष्ठा pratiṣṭhā = based, grounded in (see I.8)
वा vā = or
चिति citi = higher consciousness (see citta, I.2)
शक्ति śakti = power (see II.6)
इति iti = finis

Continuous Text: Sanskrit Transliteration and Translation

Samādhi Pādaḥ

I.1. atha-yoga-anuśāsanam

I.2. yogaś-citta-vṛtti-nirodhaḥ

I.3. tadā draṣṭuḥ sva-rūpe'vasthānam

I.4. vṛtti-sārūpyam-itaratra

I.5. vṛttayaḥ pañcatayaḥ kliṣṭa-akliṣṭāḥ

I.6. pramāṇa- viparyaya-vikalpa-nidrā-smṛtayaḥ

I.7. pratyakṣa-anumāna-āgamāḥ pramāṇāni

I.8. viparyayo mithyā-jñānam-atad-rūpa-pratiṣṭham

I.9. śabda-jñāna-anupātī vastu-śūnyo vikalpaḥ

I.10. abhāva-pratyaya-ālambanā vṛttir-nidrā

I.11. anubhūta-viṣaya-asaṃpramoṣaḥ smṛtiḥ

I.12. abhyāsa-vairāgyābhyāṃ tan-nirodhaḥ

I.13. tatra sthitau yatno'bhyāsaḥ

I.14. sa tu dīrgha-kāla-nairantarya-satkāra-āsevito dṛḍha-bhūmiḥ

I.15. dṛṣṭa-ānuśravika-viṣaya-vitṛṣṇasya vaśīkāra saṃjñā vairāgyam

I.16. tat-paraṃ puruṣa-khyāter-guṇa-vaitṛṣṇyam

I.17. vitarka-vicāra-ānanda-asmitā-anugamāt-saṃprajñātaḥ

I.18. virāma-pratyaya-abhyāsa-pūrvaḥ saṃskāra-śeṣo'nyaḥ

I.19. bhava-pratyayo videha-prakṛti-layānām

I.20. śraddhā-vīrya-smṛti-samādhi-prajñā-pūrvaka itareṣām

Samādhi Pādaḥ

I.1. Now the instruction of yoga.

I.2. Yoga is restraining the vṛttis of consciousness.

I.3. Then the dwelling of the 'see'er in his own form.

I.4. Otherwise the same form as the vṛttis [is taken by the 'See'er].

I.5. The vṛttis are fivefold distressing, [and] not distressing.

I.6. [They are] valid cognition, misconception, imagination (mental construction), sleep and memory.

I.7. Valid cognitions [are founded upon] perception, inference and testimony.

I.8. Misconception is false knowledge not based on the real form of that [object].

I.9. Mental construction or Imagination follows word knowledge and is empty of [actual] objects.

I.10. Sleep is a vṛtti supported by the notion of non-becoming.

I.11. Memory is not letting drop the experienced objetc.

I.12. Those are restrained by practice and non-attachment (detachment, dispassion).

I.13. Practice is the effort of becoming stable there.

I.14. But this [practice] becomes firmly grounded when done intensively, properly and continuously over a long period.

I.15. Vairāgya (non-attachment) is the clear-knowledge of mastery of one who is not thirsty for objects seen or heard.

I.16. The superior of that (non-attachment) is by perceiving puruṣa; then there is no thirst for the guṇas.

I.17. Wisdom [Samādhi] is accompanied by thought, reflection, bliss and 'I am'ness.

I.18. The other [Samādhi] is preceded by practicing the notion of ceasing. It has a residue only of saṃskāras.

I.19. Bhava-pratyaya [Samādhi] is of the bodiless and those absorbed in Prakṛti.

I.20. [Upāya-pratyaya samādhi] when preceded by faith, strength, memory, samādhi, and prajñā is [attained] by the others (yogīs).

I.21. tīvra-saṃvegānām-āsannaḥ

I.22. mṛdu-madhya-adhimātratvāt-tato'pi viśeṣaḥ

I.23. īśvara-praṇidhānād-vā

I.24. kleśa-karma-vipāka-āsayair-aparāmṛṣṭaḥ puruṣa-viśeṣa īśvaraḥ

I.25. tatra niratiśayaṃ sarva-jña-bījam

I.26. pūrveṣām-api guruḥ kālena-anavacchedāt

I.27. tasya vācakaḥ praṇavaḥ

I.28. taj-japas-tad-artha-bhāvanam

I.29. tataḥ pratyakcetanā-adhigamo'py-antarāya-abhāvaś-ca

I.30. vyādhi-styāna-saṃśaya-pramāda-ālasya-avirati-bhrānti-darśana-alabdha-bhūmikatva-anavasthitatvāni citta-vikṣepās-te'ntarāyāḥ

I.31. duḥkha-daurmanasya-aṅgam-ejayatva-śvāsa-praśvāsā vikṣepa-sahabhuvaḥ

I.32. tat-pratiṣedha-artham-eka-tattva-abhyāsaḥ

I.33. maitrī-karuṇā-muditā-upekṣāṇāṃ sukha-duḥkha-puṇya-apuṇya-viṣayāṇāṃ bhāvanātaś-citta-prasādanam

I.34. pracchardana-vidhāraṇābhyāṃ vā prāṇasya

I.35. viṣaya-vatī vā pravṛttir-utpannā manasaḥ sthiti-nibandhanī

I.36. viśokā vā jyotiṣmatī

I.37. vīta-rāga-viṣayaṃ vā cittam

I.38. svapna-nidrā-jñāna-ālambanaṃ vā

I.39. yathā-abhimata-dhyānād-vā

I.40. parama-aṇu-parama-mahattva-anto'sya vaśīkāraḥ

I.21. It is near for the keenly intense.

I.22. Even here there are differences because it can be mild, medium or very extreme.

I.23. Or by devotion to Īśvara.

I.24. Untouched by kleśas, karma [and its] fruit, [and its] deposits; Īśvara is a special puruṣa.

I.25. There, [in Īśvara], the seed of all knowledge is unsurpassed.

I.26. Not bound by time, [Īśvara is] also the teacher of the first [yogīs].

I.27. The word-expressing Him is the praṇava (the mantra - 'aum').

I.28. The chanting of it, the contemplation of its objective.

I.29. Then inward-mindedness is reached, and also the obstacles disappear.

I.30. Disease, apathy, doubt, carelessness, laziness, incontinence (dissipation), wandering vision, not-reaching the stages [of samādhi] and instability [in them]; these are the distractions of consciousness, these are the obstacles.

I.31. Pain, depression, trembling of the limbs, [heavy] inhalation and exhalation accompany the distractions.

I.32. The practice on one principle with the purpose of checking these.

I.33. Cultivating friendliness, kindness, gladness, and equanimity (wide-eyes) towards objects of joy, suffering, merit, or demerit [bring about] calm clarity of the consciousness.

I.34. Or by exhalation and retention of prāṇa.

I.35. Or an activity arises towards an object which binds the mind to stability.

I.36. Or by sorrowless and illuminating [activity].

I.37. Or citta (consciousness) has objects free of attachment.

I.38. Or [citta is] supported by knowledge [that comes] in dream or sleep.

I.39. Or by meditation as desired.

I.40. His mastery [spreads] from the most minute to the most immense.

I.41. kṣīṇa-vṛtter-abhijātasya-iva maṇer-grahītṛ-grahaṇa-grāhyeṣu tat-stha-tad-añjanatā samāpattiḥ

I.42. tatra śabda-artha-jñāna-vikalpaiḥ saṃkīrṇā savitarkā samāpattiḥ

I.43. smṛti-pariśuddha sva-rūpa-śūnya-iva-artha-mātra-nirbhāsā nirvitarkā

I.44. etayā-eva savicārā nirvicārā ca sūkṣma-viṣayā vyākhyātā

I.45. sūkṣma-viṣayatvaṃ ca-aliṅga-paryavasānam

I.46. tā eva sabījaḥ samādhiḥ

I.47. nirvicāra-vaiśāradye'dhyātma-prasādaḥ

I.48. ṛtaṃ-bharā tatra prajñā

I.49. śruta-anumāna-prajñābhyām-anya-viṣayā viśeṣa-arthatvāt

I.50. taj-jaḥ saṃskāro'nya-saṃskāra-pratibandhī

I.51. tasya-api nirodhe sarva-nirodhān-nirbījaḥ samādhiḥ

I.41. When the vṛttis have decreased, [the citta is] transparent like a jewel; it abides in, [and] is colored by the 'grasper, the grasping and the grasped'. This is Samāpatti.

I.42. Samāpatti with thought [occurs] where word, meaning, knowledge and imagination intermingle.

I.43. [Samāpatti] without thought [occurs where] memory is purified and is as if empty of its own form, and only the object shines forth.

I.44. By this [samāpatti] with reflection and without reflection are explained. They have subtle objects.

I.45. And the subtle object ends in the aliṅga (unmarked).

I.46. Even these are samādhi with seed.

I.47. Lucidity in [Samāpatti] without reflection - calm clarity in oneself.

I.48. There prajñā (transcendental wisdom) is truth-bearing.

I.49. The object is different from that arising from prajñā [reached] by tradition and inference, because of its specific purpose-ness.

I.50. The saṃskāra born from that impedes the other saṃskāras.

I.51. [When] also this is restrained, all is restrained. [This] is samādhi without seed.

Sādhana Pāda

II.1. tapaḥ svādhyāya-īśvara-praṇidhānāni kriyā-yogaḥ

II.2. samādhi-bhāvana-arthaḥ kleśa-tanū-karaṇa-arthaś-ca

II.3. avidyā-asmitā-rāga-dveṣa-abhiniveśāḥ pañca-kleśāḥ

II.4. avidyā kṣetram-uttareṣāṃ prasupta-tanu-vicchinnodārāṇām

II.5. anitya-aśuci-duḥkha-anātmasu nitya-śuci-sukha-ātma-khyātir avidyā

II.6. dṛg-darśana-śaktyor-eka-ātmateva-asmitā

II.7. sukha-anuśayī rāgaḥ

II.8. duḥkha-anuśayī dveṣaḥ

II.9. sva-rasa-vāhī viduṣo'pi tathā-rūḍho'bhiniveśaḥ

II.10. te pratiprasava-heyāḥ sūkṣmāḥ

II.11. dhyāna-heyās-tad-vṛttayaḥ

II.12. kleśa-mūlaḥ karma-āśayo dṛṣṭa-adṛṣṭa-janma vedanīyaḥ

II.13. sati mūle tad-vipāko jāty-āyur-bhogāḥ

II.14. te hlāda-paritāpa-phalāḥ puṇya-apuṇya-hetutvāt

II.15. pariṇāma-tāpa-saṃskāra-duḥkhair-guṇa-vṛtti-virodhāc-ca duḥkham-eva sarvaṃ vivekinaḥ

II.16. heyaṃ duḥkham-anāgatam

Sādhana Pāda

II.1. Kriyā Yoga is made of Tapas (heating disciplines), self-study and devotion to Īśvara.

II.2. With the purpose of cultivating Samādhi and with the purpose of making thin the Kleśas.

II.3. The five kleśas are not-knowing, 'I am'ness, attachment or desire, aversion or hatred, and the will-to-live (fear-of-death).

II.4. Avidyā [not-knowing] is the field of the others whether they be dormant, thinned out, interrupted or aroused.

II.5. Avidyā is envisioning the permanent, the pure, the joyful and the ātman in what is impermanent, impure, painful and not the ātman.

II.6. Asmitā [occurs] when the powers of seeing and of the seer are as if a single self.

II.7. Attachment is that which follows pleasure.

II.8. Aversion is that which follows sorrow.

II.9. The will-to-live [life instinct], flowing by its own potency, is rooted thus even in the wise ones.

II.10. These [in their] subtle [form] are overcome by involution.

II.11. Their vṛttis are overcome by meditation.

II.12. The kleśas are the root of the karma-deposit and this can be experienced in seen and unseen births.

II.13. So long as the root exists, it ripens into birth, life and bhoga.

II.14. The fruits of these are delight or anguish caused by merit or demerit.

II.15. Due to the sorrow in the process of change, in anxiety, in the saṃskāras and also due to the conflict of fluctuating guṇas - to him who discerns everything is suffering.

II.16. The suffering, which is yet to come, is to be avoided.

II.17. draṣṭṛ-dṛśyayoḥ saṃyogo heya-hetuḥ

II.18. prakāśa-kriyā-sthiti-śīlaṃ bhūta-indriya-ātmakaṃ bhoga-apavarga-arthaṃ dṛśyam

II.19. viśeṣa-aviśeṣa-liṅga-mātra-aliṅgāni guṇa-parvāṇi

II.20. draṣṭā dṛśi-mātraḥ śuddho'pi pratyaya-anupaśyaḥ

II.21. tad-artha eva dṛśyasya-ātmā

II.22. kṛta-arthaṃ prati naṣṭam-apy-anaṣṭaṃ tad-anya-sādhāraṇatvāt

II.23. sva-svāmi-śaktyoḥ sva-rūpa-upalabdhi-hetuḥ saṃyogaḥ

II.24. tasya hetur-avidyā

II.25. tad-abhāvāt saṃyoga-abhāvo hānaṃ tad-dṛśeḥ kaivalyam

II.26. viveka-khyātir-aviplavā hāna-upāyaḥ

II.27. tasya saptadhā prānta-bhūmiḥ prajñā

II.28. yoga-aṅga-anuṣṭhānād-aśuddhi-kṣaye jñāna-dīptir-ā-viveka-khyāteḥ

II.29. yama-niyama-āsana-prāṇāyāma-pratyāhāra-dhāraṇā-dhyāna-samādhayo' ṣṭāv-aṅgāni

II.30. ahiṃsā-satya-asteya-brahmacarya-aparigrahā yamāḥ

II.31. jāti-deśa-kāla-samaya-anavacchinnāḥ sārva-bhaumā mahā-vratam

II.17. The connection of the Seer with the seen is the cause of that which is to be avoided.

II.18. The seen has the tendency of brightness, action, and stability - it is embodied in the elements and the senses and its purpose is bhoga- experience and apavarga- completion.

II.19. The divisions of the guṇas are particular, not particular, with sign and without sign.

II.20. The Seer who is but seeing, although pure, perceives notions.

II.21. The essence of the seen is for that purpose only.

II.22. Although for him whose purpose is fulfilled it disappears, it still hasn't disappeared for others since it is (the) common experience.

II.23. Saṃyoga is the cause of 'catching sight' of the true form of the powers of the owner and the owned.

II.24. Its [saṃyoga] cause is avidyā - not-knowing.

II.25. When this [avidyā] does not exist, saṃyoga does not exist; this is relinquishing - the Aloneness of seeing.

II.26. The means to relinquishing - unwavering vision (view) of discernment.

II.27. For him on the last step there is prajña (wisdom-insight) sevenfold.

II.28. By performing the 'limbs' of yoga, the impurities are diminished [and] the light of knowledge [reaches] unto the vision of discernment.

II.29. The eight 'limbs' are: outer directives, inner directives, posture, breath-control, sense-withdrawal, concentration, meditation and samādhi.

II.30. The yamas (outer directives) are non-harming, truthfulness, non-stealing, continence and non-greed.

II.31. This is the great universal vow unconditioned by birth, place, time and circumstance.

II.32. śauca-saṃtoṣa-tapaḥ-svādhyāya-īśvara-praṇidhānāni niyamāḥ

II.33. vitarka-bādhane pratipakṣa-bhāvanam

II.34. vitarkā hiṃsā-adayaḥ kṛta-kārita-anumoditā lobha-krodha-moha-pūrvakā mṛdu-madhya-adhimātrā duḥkha-ajñāna-ananta-phalā iti pratipakṣa-bhāvanam

II.35. ahiṃsā-pratiṣṭhāyāṃ tat-saṃnidhau vaira-tyāgaḥ

II.36. satya-pratiṣṭhāyāṃ kriyā-phala-āśrayatvam

II.37. asteya-pratiṣṭhāyāṃ sarva-ratna-upasthānam

II.38. brahmacarya-pratiṣṭhāyāṃ vīrya-lābhaḥ

II.39. aparigraha-sthairye janma-kathaṃtā-saṃbodhaḥ

II.40. śaucāt sva-aṅga-jugupsā parair-asaṃsargaḥ

II.41. sattva-śuddhi-saumanasya-eka-agrya-indriya-jaya-ātma-darśana-yogyatvāni ca

II.42. saṃtoṣād-anuttamaḥ sukha-lābhaḥ

II.43. kāya-indriya-siddhir-aśuddhi-kṣayāt-tapasaḥ

II.44. svādhyāyād-iṣṭa-devatā-saṃprayogaḥ

II.45. samādhi-siddhir-īśvara-praṇidhānāt

II.46. sthira-sukham-āsanam

II.47. prayatna-śaithilya-ananta-samāpattibhyām

II.48. tato dvandva-anabhighātaḥ

II.32. The niyamas (inner directives) are cleanliness, contentment, tapas, self-study and devotion to Īshvara.

II.33. Removing thoughts - by the cultivation of the opposite.

II.34. Thoughts of harming and so on, whether done or caused to be done or approved; whether preceded by greed, anger or delusion; whether they be mild, moderate or intense - their endless fruits are suffering and lack of knowledge (ajñāna). Therefore - cultivation of the opposite.

II.35. Near one who is grounded in non-harming, hostility is abandoned.

II.36. When [one is] grounded in truth, actions and their fruit are connected [to one's words].

II.37. When grounded in 'abstaining from theft' all jewels come [to one].

II.38. When grounded in brahmacarya (continence), vigor is attained.

II.39. When stable in non-greed, the understanding of the 'why'ness of one's birth.

II.40. As a result of cleanliness there is disgust for one's own limbs and no intercourse with others.

II.41. [Also] purity of sattva [lucidity], cheerfulness, one-pointedness, mastery of the senses and the ability of seeing one's self.

II.42. Through contentment, the attainment of unsurpassed joy.

II.43. Through the dwindling of impurities by tapas, Siddhis in the body and the senses.

II.44. Through self-study, connection with the chosen deity.

II.45. Through devotion to Īśvara, the siddhi of samādhi.

II.46. The āsana (posture) is stable and pleasant.

II.47. By relaxation of effort and by samāpatti with the infinite.

II.48. Then [the practitioner is] untroubled by the pairs of opposites.

II.49. tasmin-sati śvāsa-praśvāsayor-gati-vicchedaḥ prāṇāyāmaḥ

II.50. bāhya-abhyantara-stambha-vṛttir-deśa-kāla-saṃkhyābhiḥ paridṛṣṭo dīrgha-sūkṣmaḥ

II.51. bāhya-abhyantara-viṣaya-ākṣepī caturthaḥ

II.52. tataḥ kṣīyate prakāśa-āvaraṇam

II.53. dhāraṇāsu ca yogyatā manasaḥ

II.54. sva-viṣaya-asaṃprayoge cittasya sva-rūpa-anukāra iva-indriyāṇāṃ pratyāhāraḥ

II.55. tataḥ paramā vaśyatā-indriyāṇām

II.49. When this is so, then prāṇāyāma (breath-control) - the cutting off of the movement of inhalation and exhalation.

II.50. Its vṛtti is external, internal or stopped; it is observed by [categories of] place, time and number and is prolonged and subtle.

II.51. The fourth goes beyond the external and internal sphere.

II.52. Then the covering of the bright light fades away.

II.53. And the mind is fit for concentration.

II.54. Pratyāhāra (sense withdrawal) is as if the senses are imitating the true form of the consciousness, by disuniting from their objects.

II.55. Then the highest control of the senses.

Vibhūti Pādaḥ

III.1. deśa-bandhaś-cittasya dhāraṇā

III.2. tatra pratyaya-ekatānatā dhyānam

III.3. tad-eva-artha-mātra-nirbhāsaṃ sva-rūpa-śūnyam-iva samādhiḥ

III.4. trayam-ekatra saṃyamaḥ

III.5. taj-jayāt prajñā-ālokaḥ

III.6. tasya bhūmiṣu viniyogaḥ

III.7. trayam-antar-aṅgaṃ pūrvebhyaḥ

III.8. tad-api bahir-aṅgaṃ nirbījasya

III.9. vyutthāna-nirodha-saṃskārayor-abhibhava-prādur-bhāvau nirodha-kṣaṇa-citta-anvayo nirodha-pariṇāmaḥ

III.10. tasya praśānta-vāhitā saṃskārāt

III.11. sarva-arthatā-ekāgratayoḥ kṣaya-udayau cittasya samādhi-pariṇāmaḥ

III.12. tataḥ punaḥ śānta-uditau tulya-pratyayau cittasya-ekāgratā-pariṇāmaḥ

III.13. etena bhūta-indriyeṣu dharma-lakṣaṇa-avasthā-pariṇāmā vyākhyātāḥ

III.14. śānta-udita-avyapadeśya-dharma-anupātī dharmī

III.15. krama-anyatvaṃ pariṇāma-anyatve hetuḥ

III.16. pariṇāma-traya-saṃyamād-atīta-anāgata-jñānam

Vibhūti Pādaḥ

III.1. Dhāraṇā (concentration) is binding consciousness to a place.

III.2. Dhyāna (meditation) is one pointed fixing of a notion there [at that place].

III.3. Samādhi is when that shines forth as the object only, as if empty of its own form.

III.4. The three together - saṃyama.

III.5. By mastery of that, the light of prajñā.

III.6. Its application is by stages.

III.7. These three limbs are inner, [in relation to] the previous.

III.8. Even so, they are external limbs [in relation to] the seedless [samādhi].

III.9. The saṃskāras of outwardness are overpowered and the saṃskāras of restraint appear. Then a moment of restraint of the consciousness. This is followed by nirodha pariṇāma - restraint transformation.

III.10. Through these saṃskāras the peaceful flow of that [consciousness].

III.11. When there is weakening of [attention to] all objects and the rise of one-pointedness, then samādhi pariṇāma, the samādhi transformation of consciousness.

III.12. Then again, when the calming down and rising notions become alike, then ekāgratā pariṇāma - the one-pointedness transformation of consciousness.

III.13. By this the transformations of dharma (characteristic), lakṣaṇa (time aspect) and avasthā (state) in the senses and elements are explained.

III.14. The dharmin (substance) follows the calming down, rising, and undetermined dharma.

III.15. The reason for the difference of the transformation is the difference of sequence.

III.16. By saṃyama on the three transformations - the knowledge of past and future.

III.17. śabda-artha-pratyayānām-itara-itara-adhyāsāt-saṃkaras-tat-pravibhāga-saṃyamāt-sarva-bhūta-ruta-jñānam

III.18. saṃskāra-sākṣāt-karaṇāt-pūrva-jāti-jñānam

III.19. pratyayasya para-citta-jñānam

III.20. na ca tat-sa-ālambanaṃ tasya-aviṣayī-bhūtatvāt

III.21. kāya-rūpa-saṃyamāt-tad-grāhya-śakti-stambhe cakṣuḥ-prakāśa-asaṃyoge'ntardhānam

III.22. sa-upakramaṃ nir-upakramaṃ ca karma tat-saṃyamād-apara-anta-jñānam-ariṣṭebhyo vā

III.23. maitry-ādiṣu balāni

III.24. baleṣu hasti-bala-ādīni

III.25. pravṛtty-āloka-nyāsāt sūkṣma-vyavahita-viprakṛṣṭa-jñānam

III.26. bhuvana-jñānaṃ sūrye saṃyamāt

III.27. candre tārā-vyūha-jñānam

III.28. dhruve tad-gati-jñānam

III.29. nābhi-cakre kāya-vyūha-jñānam

III.30. kaṇṭha-kūpe kṣut-pipāsā-nivṛttiḥ

III.31. kūrma-nāḍyāṃ sthairyam

III.32. mūrdha-jyotiṣi siddha-darśanam

III.17. [There is a natural] mixing up of word, [intended] object and notion, as they are imposed one upon the other. By saṃyama on them seperately - knowledge of the languages of all living beings.

III.18. By direct perception of saṃskāras - knowledge of previous births.

III.19. By [direct perception] of his notion - knowledge of the consciousness of another.

III.20. But it (knowledge) doesn't have that [notion] together with its base, that object being absent [from the field of saṃyama].

III.21. By saṃyama on the body's form and by stopping the power of it's being perceived, by disconnecting the light [shining from the body] to the eye - invisibility.

III.22. Karma is close by or far away. By saṃyama upon it, or by omens - the knowledge of [the] most extreme end (death).

III.23. [By saṃyama] on friendliness and so on - powers.

III.24. [By saṃyama] on powers - power as of an elephant and so on.

III.25. By directing the light of [mental] activity - the knowledge of the subtle, the concealed and the distant.

III.26. By saṃyama on the sun - knowledge of the universe.

III.27. [By saṃyama] on the moon - knowledge of the arrangements of the stars.

III.28. [By saṃyama] on the pole star - knowledge of their course.

III.29. [By saṃyama] on the navel-wheel - knowledge of the structure of the body.

III.30. [By saṃyama] on the hollow of the throat, the cessation of hunger and thirst.

III.31. [By saṃyama] on the turtle-nāḍi - stability

III.32. [By saṃyama] on the light of the head - sight of the siddhas.

III.33. prātibhād-vā sarvam

III.34. hṛdaye citta-saṃvit

III.35. sattva-puruṣayor-atyanta-asaṃkīrṇayoḥ pratyaya-aviśeṣo bhogaḥ para-arthatvāt sva-artha-saṃyamāt puruṣa-jñānam

III.36. tataḥ prātibha-śrāvaṇa-vedanā-ādarśa-āsvāda-vārtā jāyante

III.37. te samādhāv-upasargā vyutthāne siddhayaḥ

III.38. bandha-kāraṇa-śaithilyāt-pracāra-saṃvedanāc-ca cittasya para-śarīra-āveśaḥ

III.39. udāna-jayāj-jala-paṅka-kaṇṭaka-ādiṣv-asaṅga utkrāntiś-ca

III.40. samāna-jayāj-jvalanam

III.41. śrotra-ākāśayoḥ saṃbandha-saṃyamād-divyaṃ śrotram

III.42. kāya-ākāśayoḥ saṃbandha-saṃyamāl-laghu-tūla-samāpatteś-ca-ākāśa-gamanam

III.43. bahir-akalpitā vṛttir-mahā-videha tataḥ prakāśa-āvaraṇa-kṣayaḥ

III.44. sthūla-sva-rūpa-sūkṣma-anvaya-arthavattva-saṃyamād-bhūta-jayaḥ

III.45. tato'ṇima-ādi-prādur-bhāvaḥ kāya-saṃpat-tad-dharma

anabhighātaś-ca

III.46. rūpa-lāvaṇya-bala-vajra-saṃhananatvāni kāya-saṃpat

III.33. Or by prātibha (intuition) - [knowledge] of all.

III.34. [By saṃyama] on the heart - the understanding of consciousness.

III.35. Bhoga is a notion that doesn't distinguish between puruṣa and sattva, which are absolutely unmixable. By saṃyama on that which is for its own purpose, from that whose purpose is for the other - knowledge of puruṣa.

III.36. Thus arise intuition and [a heightened sense of] hearing, sensing, seeing, tasting and smelling.

III.37. These are obstacles in samādhi but siddhis in an outward state.

III.38. By loosening the causes of (bandha) being bound, and by perceiving-sensing the going-ons of the citta (consciousness), [consciousness] can enter another's body.

III.39. By mastery of the udāna [vayu], not clinging to water, mud, thorns etc., and ascending beyond [them].

III.40. By mastery of the samāna [vayu] - radiance.

III.41. By saṃyama on the relationship between the ear and the space [within it] - the divine ear.

III.42. By saṃyama on the relationship between the body and the space [surrounding it] and by samāpatti with [objects] light as cotton - walking in space.

III.43. The great 'bodiless' is an unimagined and outer vṛtti. By it, the covering of the bright light fades away.

III.44. By saṃyama on the gross, the true form, the subtle, the connectedness and the purposefulness - mastery over the elements.

III.45. Then [siddhis] such as atomization, etc., come about and there is perfection of the body and the unassailabilty of its characteristics.

III.46. The perfection of the body - beautiful form, grace, power and the compactness of a thunderbolt.

III.47. grahaṇa-sva-rūpa-asmitā-anvaya-arthavattva-saṃyamād-indriya-jayaḥ

III.48. tato mano-javitvaṃ vikaraṇa-bhāvaḥ pradhāna-jayaś-ca

III.49. sattva-puruṣa-anyatā-khyāti-mātrasya sarva-bhāva-adhiṣṭhātṛtvaṃ sarva-jñātṛtvaṃ ca

III.50. tad-vairāgyād-api doṣa-bīja-kṣaye kaivalyam

III.51 sthāny-upanimantraṇe saṅga-smaya-akaraṇaṃ punar-aniṣṭa-prasaṅgāt

III.52. kṣaṇa-tat-kramayoḥ saṃyamād-viveka-jaṃ jñānam

III.53. jāti-lakṣaṇa-deśair-anyatā-anavacchedāt-tulyayos-tataḥ pratipattiḥ

III.54. tārakaṃ sarva-viṣayaṃ sarvathā-viṣayam-akramaṃ ca-iti viveka-jaṃ jñānam

III.55. sattva-puruṣayoḥ śuddhi-sāmye kaivalyam-iti

III.47. By saṃyama on grasping, the true form, 'I am'ness', connectedness and purposefulness - mastery over the senses.

III.48. By this speed as of the mind, a state lacking sense organs and mastery of the essential components of the universe.

III.49. By merely perceiving the otherness of sattva and puruṣa, supremacy over all states of existence and all knowledge.

III.50. By non-attachment even to that, the seeds of defects diminishing, then kaivalya - aloneness.

III.51. Even then with the invitation of high placed [beings], there is no cause for attachment or pride because of the undesired and repeated inclination [of falling].

III.52. By saṃyama on the moment and the sequence - the knowledge born of discernment.

III.53. Then the ability to differentiate between those that seem the same because they cannot be distinguished by birth, temporal quality or point in space.

III.54. The knowledge born of discernment is the deliverer - all objects and all time are its objective and it is without sequence.

III.55. When the sattva and the puruṣa are of the same purity - kaivalya, aloneness.

Kaivalya Pāda

IV.1. janma-oṣadhi-mantra-tapaḥ-samādhi-jāḥ siddhayaḥ

IV.2. jāty-antara-pariṇāmaḥ prakṛty-āpūrāt

IV.3. nimittam-aprayojakaṃ prakṛtīnāṃ varaṇa-bhedas-tu tataḥ kṣetrikavat

IV.4. nirmāṇa-cittāny-asmitā-mātrāt

IV.5. pravṛtti-bhede prayojakaṃ cittam-ekam-anekeṣām

IV.6. tatra dhyāna-jam-anāśayam

IV.7. karma-aśukla-akṛṣṇaṃ yoginas-trividham-itareṣām

IV.8. tatas-tad-vipāka-anuguṇānām-eva-abhivyaktir-vāsanānām

IV.9. jāti-deśa-kāla-vyavahitānām-apy-ānantaryaṃ smṛti-saṃskārayor-eka-rūpatvat

IV.10. tāsām-anāditvaṃ ca-āśiṣo nityatvāt

IV.11. hetu-phala-āśraya-ālambanaiḥ saṃgṛhītatvād-eṣām-abhāve tad-abhāvaḥ

IV.12. atīta-anāgataṃ sva-rūpato'sty-adhva-bhedād-dharmāṇām

IV.13. te vyakta-sūkṣmā guṇa-ātmānaḥ

IV.14. pariṇāma-ekatvād-vastu-tattvam

IV.15. vastu-sāmye citta-bhedāt-tayor-vibhaktaḥ panthāḥ

IV.16. na ca-eka-citta-tantraṃ vastu tad-apramāṇakaṃ tadā kiṃ syāt

IV.17. tad-uparāga-apekṣitvāc-cittasya vastu jñāta-ajñātam

IV.18. sadā jñātās-citta-vṛttayas-tat-prabhoḥ puruṣasya-apariṇāmitvāt

Kaivalya Pāda

IV.1. The siddhis are the result of birth, herbs, mantra, tapas and samādhi.

IV.2. The transformation into another type of existence [is possible] because of nature's abundance.

IV.3. The instrumental cause does not impel nature's [evolving], it only makes a breach in the barrier as the farmer does [for irrigating his field].

IV.4. Created consciousnesses result from 'I am'ness only.

IV.5. There are distinct activities, yet it is one consciousness that impels the many.

IV.6. That which is born of meditation leaves no deposit.

IV.7. The karma of yogis is neither white nor black. The other's [karma] is of three kinds.

IV.8. Therefore, the manifestation of only those vāsanās which correspond to the ripening of [their karma].

IV.9. Because of uniformity between memory and saṃskāras there is (a) sequential relation [of karmic cause and effect] even if they are separated by birth, place and time.

IV.10. And these have no beginning because desire is eternal.

IV.11. They are held together by cause and effect, substratum and support. If these cease to be then those cease to be.

IV.12. Past and future exist in their own form because of the differences in the paths of dharma.

IV.13. These are manifest or subtle and have the nature of the guṇas.

IV.14. The 'that'ness of a thing is due to the singularity of its transformation.

IV.15. While the thing [remains] the same, consciousnesses are different, therefore the paths of these are separate.

IV.16. 'A thing is not dependent on one consciousness' - This is un-provable. If this was so, what would it [the thing] be?

IV.17. Depending on consciousness's expectation of being colored by it, a thing is known or not known.

IV.18. The vṛttis of the consciousness are always known to its master, the puruṣa, which is unchanging.

IV.19. na tat-sva-ābhāsaṃ dṛśyatvāt

IV.20. eka-samaye ca-ubhaya-anavadhāraṇam

IV.21. citta-antara-dṛśye buddhi-buddher-atiprasaṅgaḥ smṛti-saṃkaraś-ca

IV.22. citer-apratisaṃkramāyās-tad-ākāra-āpattau sva-buddhi-saṃvedanam

IV.23. draṣṭṛ-dṛśya-uparaktaṃ cittaṃ sarva-artham

IV.24. tad-asaṃkhyeya-vāsanābhiś-citram-api para-arthaṃ saṃhatya-kāritvāt

IV.25. viśeṣa-darśina ātma-bhāva-bhāvanā-vinivṛttiḥ

IV.26. tadā viveka-nimnaṃ kaivalya-prāgbhāraṃ cittam

IV.27. tac-chidreṣu pratyaya-antarāṇi saṃskārebhyaḥ

IV.28. hānam-eṣāṃ kleśavad-uktam

IV.29. prasaṃkhyāne'py-akusīdasya sarvathā viveka-khyāter-dharma-meghaḥ samādhiḥ

IV.30. tataḥ kleśa-karma-nivṛttiḥ

IV.31. tadā sarva-āvaraṇa-mala-apetasya jñānasya-ānantyāj-jñeyam-alpam

IV.32. tataḥ kṛta-arthānāṃ pariṇāma-krama-samāptir-guṇānām

IV.33. kṣaṇa-pratiyogī pariṇāma-apara-anta-nirgrāhyaḥ kramaḥ

IV.34. puruṣa-artha-śūnyānāṃ guṇānāṃ pratiprasavaḥ kaivalyaṃ sva-rūpa-pratiṣṭhā vā citi-śaktir-iti

IV.19. It (consciousness) does not shine of itself because it is the seen.
IV.20. And there cannot be a comprehending of both at the same time.
IV.21. If consciousness was seen by another, there would be excessive connectiveness between one awareness and another awareness and confusion of memory.
IV.22. There is knowledge of one's own awareness (buddhi) when the unroaming higher consciousness takes on that appearance [of consciousness].
IV.23. When the consciousness is colored by the see'er and the seen [it perceives] all objectives.
IV.24. That [consciousness], though spotted by countless (vāsanās) latent-impressions, exists for another purpose. It functions by combinations (with others, like senses, objects).
IV.25. For him who sees the distinction [between sattva and puruṣa] there is a ceasing of contemplation concerning his own states of being.
IV.26. Then consciousness is inclined towards viveka and is leaning towards aloneness.
IV.27. In the gaps, other notions from the saṃskāras [arise].
IV.28. Their relinquishing, as explained [concerning] the kleśas.
IV.29. For him who is uninterested, even in being elevated, [having] always the vision of discernment; the 'cloud of dharma' samādhi.
IV.30. Then the ceasing of the kleśas and the karma.
IV.31. Then, when all the covers of impurity have been removed - endlessness of knowledge- There is little [left] to be known.
IV.32. Then as the guṇas having fulfilled their purpose, the sequences of their transformation [come to] an end.
IV.33. The sequence is correlated to the moment and is grasped as such at the final end of transformation.
IV.34. Kaivalya (aloneness) is the involution of the guṇas [because they are] devoid of purpose for the puruṣa, or it is the grounding of the power of higher consciousness in its own form. Finis.

Continuous Text: in Devanagri script

समाधिपादः

अथ योगानुशासनम् ॥ १ । १ ॥

योगश्चित्तवृत्तिनिरोधः ॥ १ । २ ॥

तदा द्रष्टुः स्वरूपेऽवस्थानम् ॥ १ । ३ ॥

वृत्तिसारूप्यमितरत्र ॥ १ । ४ ॥

वृत्तयः पञ्चतय्यः क्लिष्टाक्लिष्टाः ॥ १ । ५ ॥

प्रमाणविपर्ययविकल्पनिद्रास्मृतयः ॥ १ । ६ ॥

प्रत्यक्षानुमानागमाः प्रमाणानि ॥ १ । ७ ॥

विपर्ययो मिथ्याज्ञानमतद्रूपप्रतिष्ठम् ॥ १ । ८ ॥

शब्दज्ञानानुपाती वस्तुशून्यो विकल्पः ॥ १ । ९ ॥

अभावप्रत्ययालम्बना वृत्तिर्निद्रा ॥ १ । १० ॥

अनुभूतविषयासंप्रमोषः स्मृतिः ॥ १ । ११ ॥

अभ्यासवैराग्याभ्यां तन्निरोधः ॥ १ । १२ ॥

तत्र स्थितौ यत्नोऽभ्यासः ॥ १ । १३ ॥

सा तु दीर्घकालनैरन्तर्यसत्कारासेवितो दृढभूमिः ॥ १ । १४ ॥

दृष्टानुश्रविकविषयवितृष्णस्य वशीकारसंज्ञा वैराग्यम् ॥ १ । १५ ॥

तत्परं पुरुषख्यातेर्गुणवैतृष्ण्यम् ॥ १ । १६ ॥

वितर्कविचारानन्दास्मितानुगमात्संप्रज्ञातः ॥ १ । १७ ॥

विरामप्रत्ययाभ्यासपूर्वः संस्कारशेषोऽन्यः ॥ १ । १८ ॥

भवप्रत्ययो विदेहप्रकृतिलयानाम् ॥ १ । १९ ॥

श्रद्धावीर्यस्मृतिसमाधिप्रज्ञापूर्वक इतरेषाम् ॥ १ । २० ॥

तीव्रसंवेगानामासन्नः ॥ १ । २१ ॥

मृदुमध्याधिमात्रत्वात्ततोऽपि विशेषः ॥ १ । २२ ॥

ईश्वरप्रणिधानाद्वा ॥ १ । २३ ॥

क्लेशकर्मविपाकासयैरपरामृष्टः पुरुषविशेष ईश्वरः ॥ १ । २४ ॥

तत्र निरतिशयं सर्वज्ञबीजम् ॥ १ । २५ ॥

पूर्वेषामपि गुरुः कालेनानवच्छेदात् ॥ १ । २६ ॥

तस्य वाचकः प्रणवः ॥ १ । २७ ॥

तज्जपस्तदर्थभावनम् ॥ १ । २८ ॥

ततः प्रत्यक्चेतनाधिगमोऽप्यन्तरायाभावश्च ॥ १ । २९ ॥

व्याधिस्त्यानसंशयप्रमादालस्याविरतिभ्रान्तिदर्शनालब्धभूमिकत्वानव
स्थितत्वानि चित्तविक्षेपास्तेऽन्तरायाः ॥ १ । ३० ॥

दुःखदौर्मनस्याङ्गमेजयत्वश्वासप्रश्वासा विक्षेपसहभुवः ॥ १ । ३१ ॥

तत्प्रतिषेधार्थमेकतत्त्वाभ्यासः ॥ १ । ३२ ॥

मैत्रीकरुणामुदितोपेक्षाणां सुखदुःखपुण्यापुण्यविषयाणां
भावनातश्चित्तप्रसादनम् ॥ १ । ३३ ॥

प्रच्छर्दनविधारणाभ्यां वा प्राणस्य ॥ १ । ३४ ॥

विषयवती वा प्रवृत्तिरुत्पन्ना मनसः स्थितिनिबन्धनी ॥ १ । ३५ ॥

विशोका वा ज्योतिष्मती ॥ १ । ३६ ॥

वीतरागविषयं वा चित्तम् ॥ १ । ३७ ॥

स्वप्ननिद्राज्ञानालम्बनं वा ॥ १ । ३८ ॥

यथाभिमतध्यानाद्वा ॥ १ । ३९ ॥

परमाणुपरममहत्त्वान्तोऽस्य वशीकारः ॥ १ । ४० ॥

क्षीणवृत्तेरभिजातस्येव मणेर्ग्रहीतृग्रहणग्राह्येषु तत्स्थतदञ्जनता
समापत्तिः ॥ १ । ४१ ॥

तत्र शब्दार्थज्ञानविकल्पैः संकीर्णा सवितर्का समापत्तिः ॥ १ । ४२ ॥

स्मृतिपरिशुद्धौ स्वरुपशून्येवार्थमात्रनिर्भासा निर्वितर्का ॥ १ । ४३ ॥

एतयैव सविचारा निर्विचारा च सूक्ष्मविषया व्याख्याता ॥ १ । ४४ ॥

सूक्ष्मविषयत्वं चालिङ्गपर्यवसानम् ॥ १ । ४५ ॥

ता एव सबीजः समाधिः ॥ १ । ४६ ॥

निर्विचारवैशारद्येऽध्यात्मप्रसादः ॥ १ । ४७ ॥

ऋतंभरा तत्र प्रज्ञा ॥ १ । ४८ ॥

श्रुतानुमानप्रज्ञाभ्यामन्यविषया विशेषार्थत्वात् ॥ १ । ४९ ॥

तज्जः संस्कारोऽन्यसंस्कारप्रतिबन्धी ॥ १ । ५० ॥

तस्यापि निरोधे सर्वनिरोधान्निर्बीजः समाधिः ॥ १ । ५१ ॥

साधनपादः

तपः स्वाध्यायेश्वरप्रणिधानानि क्रियायोगः ॥ २। १॥

समाधिभावनार्थः क्लेशतनूकरणार्थश्च ॥ २। २॥

अविद्यास्मितारागद्वेषाभिनिवेशाः पञ्चक्लेशाः ॥ २। ३॥

अविद्या क्षेत्रमुत्तरेषां प्रसुप्ततनुविच्छिन्नोदाराणाम् ॥ २। ४॥

अनित्याशुचिदुःखानात्मसु नित्यशुचिसुखात्मख्यातिरविद्या ॥ २। ५॥

दृग्दर्शनशक्त्योरेकात्मतेवास्मिता ॥ २। ६॥

सुखानुशयी रागः ॥ २। ७॥

दुःखानुशयी द्वेषः ॥ २। ८॥

स्वरसवाही विदुषोऽपि तथारूढोऽभिनिवेशः ॥ २। ९॥

ते प्रतिप्रसवहेयाः सूक्ष्माः ॥ २। १०॥

ध्यानहेयास्तद्वृत्तयः ॥ २। ११॥

क्लेशमूलः कर्माशयो दृष्टादृष्टजन्मवेदनीयः ॥ २। १२॥

सति मूले तद्विपाको जात्यायुर्भोगाः ॥ २। १३॥

ते ह्लादपरितापफलाः पुण्यापुण्यहेतुत्वात् ॥ २। १४॥

परिणामतापसंस्कारदुःखैर्गुणवृत्तिविरोधच्च दुःखमेव सर्वं विवेकिनः ॥ २ । १५ ॥

हेयं दुःखमनागतम् ॥ २ । १६ ॥

द्रष्टृदृश्ययोः संयोगो हेयहेतुः ॥ २ । १७ ॥

प्रकाशक्रियास्थितिशीलं भूतेन्द्रियात्मकं भोगापवर्गार्थं दृश्यम् ॥ २ । १८ ॥

विशेषाविशेषलिङ्गमात्रालिङ्गानि गुणपर्वाणि ॥ २ । १९ ॥

द्रष्टा दृशिमात्रः शुद्धोऽपि प्रत्ययानुपश्यः ॥ २ । २० ॥

तदर्थ एव दृश्यस्यात्मा ॥ २ । २१ ॥

कृतार्थं प्रति नष्टमप्यनष्टं तदन्यसाधारणत्वात् ॥ २ । २१ ॥

स्वस्वामिशक्त्योः स्वरूपोपलब्धिहेतुः संयोगः ॥ २ । २३ ॥

तस्य हेतुरविद्या ॥ २ । २४ ॥

तदभावात् संयोगाभावो हानं तद्दृशेः कैवल्यम् ॥ २ । २५ ॥

विवेकख्यातिरविप्लवा हानोपायः ॥ २ । २६ ॥

तस्य सप्तधा प्रान्तभूमिः प्रज्ञा ॥ २ । २७ ॥

योगाङ्गानुष्ठानादशुद्धिक्षये ज्ञानदीप्तिराविवेकख्यातेः ॥ २ । २८ ॥

यमनियमासनप्राणायामप्रत्याहारधारणाध्यानसमाधयोऽष्टावङ्गानि

॥ २। २९॥

अहिंसासत्यास्तेयब्रह्मचर्यापरिग्रहा यमाः ॥ २। ३०॥

जातिदेशकालसमयानवच्छिन्नाः सार्वभौमा महाव्रतम् ॥ २। ३१॥

शौचसंतोषतपःस्वाध्यायेश्वरप्रणिधानानि नियमाः ॥ २। ३२॥

वितर्कबाधने प्रतिपक्षभावनम् ॥ २। ३३॥

वितर्का हिंसादयः कृतकारितानुमोदिता लोभक्रोधमोहपूर्वका
मृदुमध्याधिमात्रा दुःखाज्ञानानन्तफला इति प्रतिपक्षभावनम् ॥ २। ३४॥

अहिंसाप्रतिष्ठायां तत्संनिधौ वैरत्यागः ॥ २। ३५॥

सत्यप्रतिष्ठायां क्रियाफलाश्रयत्वम् ॥ २। ३६॥

अस्तेयप्रतिष्ठायां सर्वरत्नोपस्थानम् ॥ २। ३७॥

ब्रह्मचर्यप्रतिष्ठायां वीर्यलाभः ॥ २। ३८॥

अपरिग्रहस्थैर्ये जन्मकथंतासंबोधः ॥ २। ३९॥

शौचात् स्वाङ्गजुगुप्सा परैरसंसर्गः ॥ २। ४०॥

सत्त्वशुद्धिसौमनस्यैकाग्र्येन्द्रियजयात्मदर्शनयोग्यत्वानि च ॥ २। ४१॥

संतोषादनुत्तमः सुखलाभः ॥ २। ४२॥

कायेन्द्रियसिद्धिरशुद्धिक्षयात्तपसः ॥ २। ४३॥

स्वाध्यायादिष्टदेवतासंप्रयोगः ॥ २ । ४४ ॥

समाधिसिद्धिरीश्वरप्रणिधानात् ॥ २ । ४५ ॥

स्थिरसुखमासनम् ॥ २ । ४६ ॥

प्रयत्नशैथिल्यानन्तसमापत्तिभ्याम् ॥ २ । ४७ ॥

ततो द्वन्द्वानभिघातः ॥ २ । ४८ ॥

तस्मिन्सति श्वासप्रश्वासयोर्गतिविच्छेदः प्राणायामः ॥ २ । ४९ ॥

बाह्याभ्यन्तरस्तम्भवृत्तिर्देशकालसंख्याभिः परिदृष्टो दीर्घसूक्ष्मः ॥ २ । ५० ॥

बाह्याभ्यन्तरविषयाक्षेपी चतुर्थः ॥ २ । ५१ ॥

ततः क्षीयते प्रकाशावरणम् ॥ २ । ५२ ॥

धारणासु च योग्यता मनसः ॥ २ । ५३ ॥

स्वविषयासंप्रयोगे चित्तस्य स्वरूपानुकार इवेन्द्रियाणां प्रत्याहारः ॥ २ । ५४ ॥

ततः परमा वश्यतेन्द्रियाणाम् ॥ २ । ५५ ॥

विभूतिपादः

देशबन्धश्चित्तस्य धारणा ॥ ३ । १ ॥

तत्र प्रत्ययैकतानता ध्यानम् ॥ ३ । २ ॥

तदेवार्थमात्रनिर्भासं स्वरूपशून्यमिव समाधिः ॥ ३ । ३ ॥

त्रयमेकत्र संयमः ॥ ३ । ४ ॥

तज्जयात् प्रज्ञालोकः ॥ ३ । ५ ॥

तस्य भूमिषु विनियोगः ॥ ३ । ६ ॥

त्रयमन्तरङ्गं पूर्वेभ्यः ॥ ३ । ७ ॥

तदपि बहिरङ्गं निर्बीजस्य ॥ ३ । ८ ॥

व्युत्थाननिरोधसंस्कारयोरभिभवप्रादुर्भावौ निरोधक्षणचित्तान्वयो
निरोधपरिणामः ॥ ३ । ९ ॥

तस्य प्रशान्तवाहिता संस्कारात् ॥ ३ । १० ॥

सर्वार्थ तैकाग्रतयोः क्षयोदयौ चित्तस्य समाधिपरिणामः ॥ ३ । ११ ॥

ततः पुनः शान्तोदितौ तुल्यप्रत्ययौ चित्तस्यैकाग्रतापरिणामः ॥ ३ । १२ ॥

एतेन भूतेन्द्रियेषु धर्मलक्षणावस्थापरिणामा व्याख्याताः ॥ ३ । १३ ॥

शान्तोदिताव्यपदेश्यधर्मानुपाती धर्मी ॥ ३। १४ ॥

क्रमान्यत्वं परिणामान्यत्वे हेतुः ॥ ३। १५ ॥

परिणामत्रयसंयमादतीतानागतज्ञानम् ॥ ३। १६ ॥

शब्दार्थप्रत्ययानामितरेतराध्यासात्संकरस्तत्प्रविभागसंयमात्सर्वभूतरुतज्ञ
ानम् ॥ ३। १७ ॥

संस्कारसाक्षात्करणात्पूर्वजातिज्ञानम् ॥ ३। १८ ॥

प्रत्ययस्य परचित्तज्ञानम् ॥ ३। १९ ॥

न च तत्सालम्बनं तस्याविषयीभूतत्वात् ॥ ३। २० ॥

कायरूपसंयमात्तद्ग्राह्यशक्तिस्तम्भे चक्षुःप्रकाशासंयोगेऽन्तर्धानम्
॥ ३। २१ ॥

सोपक्रमं निरुपक्रमं च कर्म तत्संयमादपरान्तज्ञानमरिष्टेभ्यो वा
॥ ३। २२ ॥

मैत्र्यादिषु बलानि ॥ ३। २३ ॥

बलेषु हस्तिबलादीनि ॥ ३। २४ ॥

प्रवृत्त्यालोकन्यासात् सूक्ष्मव्यवहितविप्रकृष्टज्ञानम् ॥ ३। २५ ॥

भुवनज्ञानं सूर्ये संयमात् ॥ ३। २६ ॥

चन्द्रे ताराव्यूहज्ञानम् ॥ ३ । २७ ॥

ध्रुवे तद्गतिज्ञानम् ॥ ३ । २८ ॥

नाभिचक्रे कायव्यूहज्ञानम् ॥ ३ । २९ ॥

कण्ठकूपे क्षुत्पिपासानिवृत्तिः ३ । ३० ॥

कूर्मनाड्यां स्थैर्यम् ॥ ३ । ३१ ॥

मूर्धज्योतिषि सिद्धदर्शनम् ॥ ३ । ३२ ॥

प्रातिभाद्वा सर्वम् ॥ ३ । ३३ ॥

हृदये चित्तसंवित् ॥ ३ । ३४ ॥

सत्त्वपुरुषयोरत्यन्तासंकीर्णयोः प्रत्ययाविशेषो भोगः परार्थत्वात्
स्वार्थसंयमात् पुरुषज्ञानम् ॥ ३ । ३५ ॥

ततः प्रातिभश्रावणवेदनादर्शास्वादवार्ता जायन्ते ॥ ३ । ३६ ॥

ते समाधावुपसर्गा व्युत्थाने सिद्धयः ॥ ३ । ३७ ॥

बन्धकारणशैथिल्यात्प्रचारसंवेदनाच्च चित्तस्य परशरीरावेशः ॥ ३ । ३८ ॥

उदानजयाज्जलपङ्ककण्टकादिष्वसङ्ग उत्क्रान्तिश्च ॥ ३ । ३९ ॥

समानजयाज्ज्वलनम् ॥ ३ । ४० ॥

श्रोत्राकाशयोः संबन्धसंयमाद्दिव्यं श्रोत्रम् ॥ ३ । ४१ ॥

कायाकाशयोः संबन्धसंयमाल्लघुतूलसमापत्तेश्चाकाशगमनम् ॥ ३। ४२॥

बहिरकल्पिता वृत्तिर्महाविदेह ततः प्रकाशावरणक्षयः ॥ ३। ४३॥

स्थूलस्वरूपसूक्ष्मान्वयार्थवत्त्वसंयमाद्भूतजयः ॥ ३। ४४ ॥

ततोऽणिमादिप्रादुर्भावः कायसंपत्तद्धर्मानभिघातश्च ॥ ३। ४५॥

रूपलावण्यबलवज्रसंहननत्वानि कायसंपत् ॥ ३। ४६॥

ग्रहणस्वरूपास्मितान्वयार्थवत्त्वसंयमादिन्द्रियजयः ॥ ३। ४७॥

ततो मनोजवित्वं विकरणभावः प्रधानजयश्च ॥ ३। ४८ ॥

सत्त्वपुरुषान्यताख्यातिमात्रस्य सर्वभावाधिष्ठातृत्वं सर्वज्ञातृत्वं च ॥ ३। ४९॥

तद्वैराग्यादपि दोषबीजक्षये कैवल्यम् ॥ ३। ५० ॥

स्थान्युपनिमन्त्रणे सङ्गस्मयाकरणं पुनरनिष्टप्रसङ्गात् ॥ ३। ५१॥

क्षणतत्क्रमयोः संयमाद्विवेकजं ज्ञानम् ॥ ३। ५२॥

जातिलक्षणदेशैरन्यतानवच्छेदात्तुल्ययोस्ततः प्रतिपत्तिः ॥ ३। ५३॥

तारकं सर्वविषयं सर्वथाविषयमक्रमं चेति विवेकजं ज्ञानम् ॥ ३। ५४ ॥

सत्त्वपुरुषयोः शुद्धिसाम्ये कैवल्यमिति ॥ ३। ५५॥

कैवल्य पाद

जन्मौषधिमन्त्रतपःसमाधिजाः सिद्धयः ॥ ४ । १ ॥

जात्यन्तरपरिणामः प्रकृत्यापूरात् ॥ ४ । २ ॥

निमित्तमप्रयोजकं प्रकृतीनां वरणभेदस्तु ततः क्षेत्रिकवत् ॥ ४ । ३ ॥

निर्माणचित्तान्यस्मितामात्रात् ॥ ४ । ४ ॥

प्रवृत्तिभेदे प्रयोजकं चित्तमेकमनेकेषाम् ॥ ४ । ५ ॥

तत्र ध्यानजमनाशयम् ॥ ४ । ६ ॥

कर्माशुक्लाकृष्णं योगिनस्त्रिविधमितरेषाम् ॥ ४ । ७ ॥

ततस्तद्विपाकानुगुणानामेवाभिव्यक्तिर्वासनानाम् ॥ ४ । ८ ॥

जातिदेशकालव्यवहितानामप्यानन्तर्यं स्मृतिसंस्कारयोरेकरूपत्वत् ॥ ४ । ९ ॥

तासामनादित्वं चाशिषो नित्यत्वात् ॥ ४ । १० ॥

हेतुफलाश्रयालम्बनैः संगृहीतत्वादेषामभावे तदभावः ॥ ४ । ११ ॥

अतीतानागतं स्वरूपतोऽस्त्यध्वभेदाद्धर्माणाम् ॥ ४ । १२ ॥

ते व्यसूक्ष्मा गुणात्मानः ॥ ४ । १३ ॥

परिणामैकत्वाद्वस्तुतत्त्वम् ॥ ४ । १४ ॥

वस्तुसाम्ये चित्तभेदात्तयोर्विभः पन्थाः ॥ ४ । १५ ॥

न चैकचित्ततन्त्रं वस्तु तदप्रमाणकं तदा किं स्यात् ॥ ४ । १६ ॥

तदुपरागापेक्षित्वाच्चित्तस्य वस्तु ज्ञाताज्ञातम् ॥ ४ । १७ ॥

सदा ज्ञाताश्चित्तवृत्तयस्तत्प्रभोः पुरुषस्यापरिणामित्वात् ॥ ४ । १८ ॥

न तत्स्वाभासं दृश्यत्वात् ॥ ४ । १९ ॥

एकसमये चोभयानवधारणम् ॥ ४ । २० ॥

चित्तान्तरदृश्ये बुद्धिबुद्धेरतिप्रसङ्गः स्मृतिसंकरश्च ॥ ४ । २१ ॥

चितेरप्रतिसंक्रमायास्तदाकारापत्तौ स्वबुद्धिसंवेदनम् ॥ ४ । २२ ॥

द्रष्टृदृश्योपरं चित्तं सर्वार्थम् ॥ ४ । २३ ॥

तदसंख्येयवासनाभिश्चित्रमपि परार्थं संहत्यकारित्वात् ॥ ४ । २४ ॥

विशेषदर्शिन आत्मभावभावनाविनिवृत्तिः ॥ ४ । २५ ॥

तदा विवेकनिम्नं कैवल्यप्राग्भारं चित्तम् ॥ ४ । २६ ॥

तच्छिद्रेषु प्रत्ययान्तराणि संस्कारेभ्यः ॥ ४ । २७ ॥

हानमेषां क्लेशवदुम् ॥ ४ । २८ ॥

प्रसंख्यानेऽप्यकुसीदस्य सर्वथा विवेकख्यातधर्ममेघः समाधिः
॥ ४ । २९ ॥

ततः क्लेशकर्मनिवृत्तिः ॥ ४ । ३० ॥

तदा सर्वावरणमलापेतस्य ज्ञानस्यानन्त्याज्ज्ञेयमल्पम् ॥ ४ । ३१ ॥

ततः कृतार्थानां परिणामक्रमसमाप्तिर्गुणानाम् ॥ ४ । ३२ ॥

क्षणप्रतियोगी परिणामापरान्तनिर्ग्राह्यः क्रमः ॥ ४ । ३३ ॥

पुरुषार्थशून्यानां गुणानां प्रतिप्रसवः कैवल्यं स्वरूपप्रतिष्ठा वा चितिशक्तिरिति
॥ ४ । ३४ ॥

Bibliography

Four Chapters on Freedom, Swami Satyananda Saraswati, Yoga Publication Trust, Munger, Bihar, 1976.

Light on the Yoga Sutras of Patanjali, BKS Iyengar, London: Aquarian Press, 1993.

The Yoga-Sutra of Patanjali: A New Translation and Commentary, Feuerstein, Georg, Vermont: Inner Traditions International, 1989.

The Early Upanishads, Olivelle, Patrick, trans. London: Oxford University Press, 1998.

The Rig Veda: An Anthology, Doniger, Wendy, trans. England: Penguin Books, 1981.

The Principal Upanishads, Radhakrishnan, S., trans. India: Harper Collins, 2000.

The Science of Yoga, I.K. Taimni, Theosophical Publishing House, 1979.

The Yoga-System of Patanjali, James Haughton Woods, Harvard Oriental Series, Motilal Banarsidass, 1966.

Shankara on the Yoga Sutras, Leggett, Trevor, trans. Delhi: Motilal, Banarsidass, 1982.

Yoga, Disciplne of Freedom, Barbara Stoller Miller, University of California Press, 1996.

Yogavarttika of Vijnanabhikshu, Rukmani, T.S., *trans.* New Delhi: Munshiram Manoharlal, 1987.

Suggestions for Further Reading

Aurobindo, Sri - **The Synthesis of Yoga** - Aurobindo Ashram, Pondicherry, India, 1970.

Feuerstein G. - **The Technology of Ecstasy** - Tarcher Press, 1989.

Flood, Gavin - **An Introduction to Hinduism** - Cambridge University Press, 1996.

Mascaro, J. - **The Bhagavad Gita** - Penguin Books, 1982.

Swami Nikhilananda - **The Gospel of Sri Ramakrishna** - Ramakrishna-Vivekananda Center, 1992.